THE SENSE OF INJUSTICE

THE SENSE
OF INJUSTICE

BY

EDMOND CAHN

INDIANA UNIVERSITY PRESS
BLOOMINGTON

ACKNOWLEDGMENT

"Justice and Power" and "Freedom and Order" are substantially revised versions of articles which appeared respectively in 55 Yale L. J. 336 (1946) and 23 N. Y. U. L. Q. Rev. 20 (1948). I am grateful to the *Yale Law Journal* and *New York University Law Quarterly Review* for permitting me to make use of these articles, and I am especially grateful to them for publishing the articles in the first place and thus affording me the benefit of valuable criticisms.

E. C.

CONTENTS

THE PURPOSE OF THIS BOOK

ONE OF THE MOST intriguing passages in all legendary literature deals with an incident in the life of the patriarch Jacob. We are told that, having sent his household ahead on a journey, he camped alone at the edge of a river. There a strange man came up to him as he sat beside his tent. They proceeded to wrestle with each other unremittingly all through the darkness of the night, and when the sun rose in the morning Jacob still clung to the stranger until he was able to exact a blessing from him. Thereupon this mysterious adversary vanished again into the realm of unreality. Here the narrative breaks off and we are left free to assign it whatever interpretation we choose. If, then, Jacob is taken to represent the concrete living individual, on the one hand, and the ghostly adversary is made to stand for abstraction, concept, or symbol, on the other, the struggle in this little incident epitomizes rather effectually the whole history of legal philosophy; but as yet no final blessing has been heard.

The purpose of this book is to present an anthropocentric view of the law. Since concepts and abstractions are indispensable instruments of both the regime of law and the practice of philosophy, they have understandably engrossed the attention of legal philosophers at the expense of what is vibrant, fleshly, and individual. An anthropocentric approach, far from banishing concepts, may possibly restore them to their proper dignity — as ministers of the needs and satisfactions of living persons. Legal philosophy, when it has seen fit to turn its eyes toward men, has customarily regarded them either as a row of identical pegs on which to hang rights and interests or as mere particular instances of some conceptualized being called " Man "; but, when the law of a state is infringed and someone has to be punished, is it a concept or a living person that we send to jail? The abstraction performs an effectual function in the operating machinery of law, but the ultimate consumer of the product will always be some quite concrete individual. In this book, therefore, the meaning of any concept, however exalted, is investigated by observing the occasions when that concept becomes relevant to the homely experiences of individual human beings.

Under an anthropocentric view, which concepts can be expected to cast the clearest light on the nature of law? The choice would be rather difficult if we did not have the benefit of indications visibly and repeatedly inscribed in the history of philosophy. The life of any reflective undertaking has been shown to consist in the clash and conflict of hostile principles; *i.e.*, in the persistent antitheses of the particular field. The collision of force with opposing force is what sheds flying sparks of illumination. That is why the ideal is habitually set off against the positive, identity against time, the free against the determined, reason against passion. And such a procedure is handsomely suited to the objectives of an anthropocentric view of law. To use it, we need only call up, in their respective turns, the fundamental classic antitheses of legal theory. They are: *Justice and Power, Freedom and Order, Security and Change.*

Yet law-abiding scholars write;
Law is neither wrong nor right,
Law is only crimes
Punished by places and by times. . . .
— W. H. AUDEN, *Law Like Love*

I. *The Elements*

IN THE BEGINNING there were those who believed that law was only the will of the dominant local deity, and in our own era there are those who believe that law is only the will of the dominant economic class. The question whether the difference between these beliefs constitutes a net advance may be interesting, but for immediate purposes it is less important than the fact that the two agree in defining law as a manifestation of applied power. The empirical evidence in support of this position has always been impressive.

Nevertheless, philosophers have long held the opposing opinion: that justice or righteousness is the source, the substance, and the ultimate end of law. Such a doctrine was announced at least as early as the Book of Leviticus and the masterpieces of the Athenian enlightenment. It developed under the influence of the Stoics through the centuries of decadence in the Roman republic and early empire, assumed a pseudo-Christian guise by the time of Justinian's *Corpus Juris*, flourished amid the brutalities of medieval Europe, and became, in the skillful hands of Thomas Aquinas, an authentic tenet of theology.

Early in this honorable career, the meaning of justice found itself interlaced with the philosophic systems of " natural " law. These systems regarded man — in the Aristotelian fashion — as a completely congenial member of the world of nature, and they considered his society as just one more organism to be studied in the grand movement of the cosmos. There are natural laws to govern the relations of stars and planets on their journeys through the heavenly spheres, and, by like token, there must be natural laws to govern the relations of human beings in their social and political orders. Human reason, it was assumed, could discover and human discourse could formulate these natural laws for the guidance of men. Justice then would be defined as the state of human relations that followed from conforming with the precepts of nature, once they had been ascertained. The natural laws were independent of time and place; like human rationality, they were the same always and everywhere. So too was justice; once discovered, it offered a universal and immutable formula.

In this scheme of thought, what was the role of positive law; *i.e.*, the law that the ruler decrees or the legislature enacts or the court applies to controversies as they are presented? Positive law was considered to be merely derivative. It drew its force from the principles of the higher constitutive code of natural law. It lost authority whenever it violated those principles. If it did violate them, a citizen became free to return to the elementary natural precepts and to use their authority against the mandates of his positive government. Thus natural law could be made to sanction revolutions as diverse as the British of 1688, the

American, and the French. Only a justice above positive law seemed able to rationalize the defiance of temporal power and the overthrow of tyrannical sovereigns.

The implications of these familiar doctrines go deep into property institutions, political structures, and basic civil rights. They are equally profound in the shaping of international law. Similarity of positive codes, as European history of the last century has shown, does not make for understanding or peace among nations, unless enriched and strengthened by mutual subscription to metacodal principles, such as fair dealing or adherence to pacts. Only a general sharing of the attitude of justice can support effective international law. Municipal law, though inscribed in identical terms, will mean different things on different sides of a frontier that is not merely national but moral.

In the United States, the position has been substantially affected by the adoption of a written Constitution. So long as that document was considered the engraved tablet of natural law — elemental and eternal — judges must turn to nature to find the exposition and add the gloss to the written phrases of the Constitution. The law of nature appeared to furnish some answers which were highly convenient for reactionary purposes, to have anticipated some peculiarly complex and novel issues, and too often to have favored established property interests. More recently, explicit reference to natural axioms has become rare; nature is suspect. But so much remains of the liberal principles which natural-law thinking (of the eighteenth century) conferred on the written Constitution that judges need not often look farther when they wish to keep the meaning of the Constitution abreast of social advances. This has proved comforting, for it permits the desired results to be attained without doctrinal dispute. Judges may speak of "due process," "equal protection," "general welfare," "reasonableness" — all somehow cleansed of natural rights or higher law. But would the decision be the same if twenty-four centuries had not preached an indwelling justice?

Distrust of the law of nature is predominantly modern. True, some more sophisticated of the ancients, having heard much mouthing of *ex aequo et bono*, might mutter *cui bono?* [1] — but the tide of skepticism did not rise noticeably until the seventeenth century.[2] It had been observed that the laws of nature were either too general to offer much help in concrete cases or too specific to claim universal and absolute authority.[3] Equality, for instance, might appear an inspiring maxim, but how could one determine

[1] Cicero, De re publica III. viii–xi (Loeb's trans. 1928), 193–201; Xenophon, Memorabilia I. ii (Loeb's trans. 1923), 31–35.

[2] "Justice is subject to dispute; might is easily recognised and is not disputed. So we cannot give might to justice, because might has gainsaid justice, and has declared that it is she herself who is just. And thus being unable to make what is just strong, we have made what is strong just." — Pensées de M. Pascal sur la religion et sur quelques autres sujets, No. 298.

[3] In a long series of decisions beginning soon after the Civil War and continuing with increasing frequency up to 1937, the Supreme Court's majority promoted its economic and social prejudices to the rank of immutable natural laws, in the name of which all sorts of experimental and progressive statutes were nullified. Since 1937 most of these decisions have been overruled. However, there still remain, apparently unimpeached, such vestiges of this obsolete mode of thought as Pierce v. Society of Sisters, 268 U. S. 510 (1925). In this case, the Court struck down an Oregon law requiring all children to receive their primary education at public schools only. Despite the strange unanimity of the opinion, it is a vulnerable one, because the state of Oregon demurred to the pleadings filed by the private schools, instead of answering them and offering evidence in support of the legislative policy expressed in the statute.

the equals between this particular merchant and this manufacturer, this vendor and this purchaser, this heir and this creditor? If natural law had a neat categorical principle for real property in imperial Rome, what value could that exhibit under the manorial customs of Norman England or the Soviet system of collective farms? The law is busy with individuals, with the here-and-now; it must get on with its work of answering and sending litigants away. What Thomas Aquinas or John Locke said was lofty enough, but it did not decide the case. Moreover, lawyers and judges could quote the vague maxims of the law of nature for any position whatever, for revolution and reaction, plutocracy and community of goods. Natural law might be nailed to anyone's mast. It was, in fact, so universal that it could never be found.

The heaviest blow to natural justice came, characteristically enough, from within; that is, not from denial but from reinterpretation. The author of destruction was Thomas Hobbes. Natural law is the embodiment of specific assumptions concerning the character of man, and in general draws its authority from those assumptions. If as Hobbes supposed man is by nature all cannibal — tearing, destroying, devouring except when restrained — then ultimately he must turn to sovereign force for the most elementary protection, and organized society thus becomes a technique for muzzling wolves. Natural law had posited original virtue (whether by birth or divine grace); Hobbes could find only original viciousness. Thus justice, to live at all, must seek the aegis of sovereign constraint.

From this point it was only a step to accepting power as the substance of legality. The view of man again dictated the view of law. If, as in Jeremy Bentham's system of utilitarianism, humanity is the weathercock of pleasure and pain, then legislation can keep the wind blowing in the right direction. The effectual way to serve utility is by law; that is, by the intelligent command of the sovereign. All talk of nature and natural rights was mere polemics, if not downright abuse. The law is what the organ of state power directs; and obedience is induced by promises of pleasure and, more frequently, by threats of pain. A generation after Bentham, John Austin took his analysis of law and purged it of its optimistic utilitarianism. The task of jurisprudence, said Austin, is to examine the law as a formal system of commands issued by the sovereign, who announces the sanctions that will serve to enforce his mandates.

Now law qua command seems at least to have one dialectic advantage: the command, hence the law, can presumably be found. Legislative enactments and judicial decisions are there to be read, and it matters little that Continental theorists have looked primarily to the former and Anglo-Saxons have concentrated on the latter. Different organs may speak for the sovereign; all in speaking issue commands — the only law that Austin and his followers would recognize. Each nation has its own sovereign, each sovereign utters his own commands, each set of commands represents a distinct legal system. During the past half century, as attitudes toward society and the integral man became tougher and more cynical, the command analysis has grown progressively popular. At its extreme, it has been used to rationalize every ruthlessness, every abandon and misanthropic contempt. Bentham wished man to be liberated by legislation: his insights were made to serve the ends of bondage. This, of course, did not make them false in themselves.

The doctrine has already undergone a number of refinements. In the first place, if law is command, whose command is it? The modern world seemed to offer no instance of sovereign power completely monopolized by a single individual. Everywhere, even in the most compact tyrannies, state power was divided and parceled out; in the countries that analytic jurisprudence knew best (England, the United States, and the nations of western Europe), the differentiation was perhaps greatest. The search for the unique source of the command engendered a sizeable literature on sovereignty, its nature and location, which lost in profit as it grew in size.

The command itself proved little more certain than its source. Leaving aside all question of judicial and administrative interpretation, one may still fail to discover a clear command in most rules of law. Who is commanded to do what, for example, by a statute that simply requires two witnesses for a valid will? Here was a real logical difficulty, augmented by the even graver psychological dilemma: that most law is not subjectively felt to be a command. It might be termed a hypothetical command — " If A injures B in such and such a manner, the judge shall require A to make restitution "; but the rule of law appears to be primarily a mandate to the judge (or perhaps to the sheriff). Of course, with the practice of sufficient ingenuity, declarations of very great variety can be transposed into some sort of imperatives; an artificial symmetry can be achieved. But this is mere exercise in grammar. So extended, the command theory progressively loses its productivity, as theories always do beyond the margins of convincing insight.

The position has been further weakened by its extreme nominalism. It had no way to account for the resemblances among legal systems; that is, no way in terms of an utterly capricious sovereign will. If law is not shaped by justice, ethos, the socioeconomic matrix, but by a mere series of commands, then how do the sovereigns happen so often to will the same? Of necessity, the reply would allude to similarities in economic structure and social circumstance, coincidences of history and religious faith, or participation in an ancestral juristic tradition. But, if these are the explanations, where is the free, unfettered sovereign will? It seems largely determined, as indeed it should be. A wholly free will in a finite world is a fair definition of insanity.

These troubling qualifications of Austin's doctrine, that law is sovereign command, have not led to its rejection. Instead, they have induced an attitude of extreme positivism resolved not to inquire into the principal assumptions of the theory. The business of the jurist, we are told, is to look at the law as given and to study its day-to-day operations in the courts and administrative agencies. Other considerations are matters for politics, sociology, or ethics; jurisprudence cannot solve the enigmas of justice and injustice, progress and regression, so it should be satisfied to explain the law in terms of an existent going concern. It should describe, but not attempt to evaluate.

In the twentieth century, sheer power enjoys a respect bordering on idolatry, and legal philosophers yield freely to the general worship. We hear the cynics, the disillusioned, and the callous. We hear also the devotees of the " pure theory of law " who dismiss all " political " considerations as irrelevant because justice and such like values are " irrational " and are therefore " not subject to cognition." [4] Thus, whatever the particular pretext may be, the search for the meaning of justice appears to have been given up. The result is that irresponsible force threatens to occupy a field abandoned by those who might restrain it. Thus, in the antithesis between justice and power, the latter characteristically enough needs no expositor or advocate; it is justice that must demonstrate reality in the operations of law.

Enough has been said of the two forces to indicate their fundamental contradictions. These should serve to warn us that limited principles have been extended beyond the boundaries of validity. Now, as a fresh analysis is to be attempted,[5] expectations had better remain modest. An ancient antithesis does not easily submit to smooth neatness; it will always show a certain restiveness.

II. *The Sense of Injustice*

A Path to Justice. The stubborn survival of some sort of faith in *natural* justice should point to a nucleus of truth. Errors, whether sincere or interested, were committed by the natural-law philosophers; the pretensions of

[4] Kelsen, General Theory of Law and State 13 (1945). To agree with this reasoning, it is necessary only to disregard the greater part of the findings of modern psychology.

[5] Meaning only that an effort has been made to think matters through, without conscious borrowing. Everything here is original and very little is novel.

their systems became far too extravagant. Natural law sought to decide controversies in which it had no role and to offer absolute answers where only the tentative or relative would serve. It was guilty of the Duchess' fallacy in *Alice in Wonderland:* it insisted that everything must have a moral in a universe full of the irrelevant, the inane, the neutral, the fatuous, and the frolicsome. To make matters worse, its principles proved hopelessly discrete. The evolutionary connectedness of human life and of man's relations is the root fact of law; a collection, however ideal, of static, discontinuous maxims simply could not perform the task. Justice, as many attempted definitions have rather clearly demonstrated, is unwilling to be captured in a formula. Nevertheless, it somehow remains a word of magic evocations.

One clear occasion of these difficulties was the resort to rigorous deductive reasoning in the derivation of rules from ambitious axioms. Here it is proposed to pursue a different route. Perhaps the human mind does contain self-evident truths concerning justice, from which legal norms less obvious in their nature may be deduced; we shall, all the same, feel safer in trusting to experience and observation. What is given in experience appears, of course, less orderly and consecutive than any categorical maxim, but it at least offers a point of return in the cycle of ratiocination. As general propositions concerning law must ultimately succeed or fail in terms of their verifiable consequences, one would suppose that they can best be obtained in the very market place where they are to be realized upon. Justice is, of course, an ideal value of highest rank, but its positive embodiments are so thoroughly alloyed with other values and interests that it can never be completely refined out. Generalizing from particular rules and judgments will not assist us, for how are we to know that the instances selected are themselves wholly " just "? The lofty abstract concept lurks somewhere beyond our discernment; it offers no incarnation which may be trusted as quite unmixed and pure.

Thus we might be left entirely without empirical guidance, were it not for what we are about to call *the sense of injustice*. This sense is clearly and frequently manifested; it is a familiar and observable phenomenon. Its incidences show how justice arises and what biologic purpose it serves in human affairs.

Why do we speak of the " sense of injustice " rather than the " sense of justice "? Because " justice " has been so beclouded by natural-law writings that it almost inevitably brings to mind some ideal relation or static condition or set of preceptual standards, while we are concerned, on the contrary, with what is active, vital, and experiential in the reactions of human beings. Where justice is thought of in the customary manner as an ideal mode or condition, the human response will be merely contemplative, and contemplation bakes no loaves. But the response to a real or imagined instance of injustice is something quite different; it is alive with movement and warmth in the human organism. For this reason, the name " sense of injustice " seems much to be preferred. What then would be meant by " justice " in the context of the approach adopted in this book? The answer would appear to be: not a state, but a process; not a condition, but an action. " Justice," as we shall use the term, means the *active process* of remedying or preventing what would arouse the sense of injustice.

And now for some instances:

Instance A. Five men who had met to dine together are brought before a judge, on the complaint of the same police officer that each of them parked his automobile one hour overtime in the same block. All plead " not guilty " but offer no evidence or explanation. The testimony of the policeman is uniform regarding each alleged offense. The judge acquits three, imposes a five-dollar fine on one, and sends the fifth defendant to jail for ninety days. This evokes the sense of injustice.

Obviously, in a given ethos all five might have been acquitted; alternately, all might have been convicted and punished in some appropriate manner. Regardless of the individual dispositions, the inequalities arbitrarily created arouse the sense of injustice, because equal treatment of those similarly situated with respect to the issue before the court is a deep implicit expectation of the legal order.

Now equality is in general the creature of positive law.[6] Courts and legislatures establish classes of humanity, categorizing for one or another purpose the duties and rights they desire to effect, to destroy, or to qualify. Thus, before a court, those only are equal whom the law has elected to equalize. The point is that the inequalities resulting from the law must make sense. If decisions differ, some discernible distinction must be found bearing an intelligible relation to the difference in result. The sense of injustice revolts against whatever is unequal by caprice. The

[6] The instance given is advisedly extreme, but so extensive is the operation of positive law on this issue of equality that we should have to add that all five men were duly licensed to drive and that none of them had a previous unfavorable record.

arbitrary, though indispensable to many of law's daily operations, is always suspect; it becomes unjust when it discriminates between indistinguishables.

As human integers, men are indistinguishables. This natural fact imposes a limit on the classificatory discretion of positive law. The sense of injustice does not tolerate juridic classes by which the integral status of man is violated. Legal slavery, for example, was doomed to disappear everywhere, for no other reason than that a slave is a man. Here we recognize one of the fixed stars of an anthropocentric jurisprudence: nature has made man a prime which positive law cannot justly differentiate.

Why does the sense of injustice call actively for equality? One explanation is that equal treatment of all within a recognized class is a necessary attribute of any legal order; the very concept of law requires this minimal regularity. In terms of pure intellection, such an analysis appears quite persuasive, but it can hardly account for the sense of injustice. One does not become outraged and furious merely because some decision has violated a dialectic pattern. The true reason must go considerably deeper, below the threshold of feeling. It must make clear why the humble and illiterate, the drawers of water and hewers of wood can hate injustice with a burning hatred. The roots of this demand for equality will be exposed when we come later to describe the sense of injustice as a general phenomenon.

Instance B. Two shoe-factory employees, carrying a large amount of money, are waylaid, robbed, and fatally injured. The incident occurs during a period of intense public feeling against radicals of every kind. Subsequently, a shoemaker and a fish peddler are charged with the crime and, though entirely innocent, are convicted on flimsy circumstantial evidence. The fact that the fish peddler is an avowed anarchist influences the decisions of the trial judge, the jury, the appellate court, and an advisory commission appointed by the governor. After languishing in jail for seven years, the accused are executed. This is felt to be unjust.

Here the sense of injustice attaches itself to the notion of desert. The law is regarded as an implement for giving men what they deserve, balancing awards and punishments in the scale of merit. As *general* merit is so difficult of admeasurement, legal action is usually expected to relate to *particular* merit; that is, to the right, duty, or guilt acquired in a specific circumstance. Sometimes, because of its own clumsiness, the law cannot fulfill this function. Then it may convict a murderer for a murder he has not committed, or a gangster for failure to report his income. In such case, the legal subterfuge does not evoke a keen sense of injustice, for desert has been somehow accorded. Thus, not merely the truth or falsity of a verdict but its relation to desert is a criterion of approval.

Nothing can so heartily satisfy this sense as an incident of " poetic " justice. That he who lives by the sword shall die by the sword, who digs a pit for his neighbor shall fall therein, who builds a high gallows for the innocent shall hang thereon — all these denouements seem peculiarly fitting. But the law cannot so variously adapt the punishment to the crime; it has a limited stock of beneficences and sanctions, limited by the need of legislative control over the inventive imagination of judges. Poetic justice, rare enough as it is, is also imperfect, for the wholesale malefactor can die only once. The sense of injustice does not call for highly dramatic or individualized awards. It adjusts to familiar imperfections. What it cannot stomach is the use of law to raise up the guilty or to punish the innocent.

Instance C. The defendant is convicted of treasonable utterances by which he successfully sought to impair the morale and obedience of combat soldiers in time of war. The sentence of the court is that he be compelled to submit to a surgical operation on his vocal chords, so that thereafter he may only bark like a dog. This affronts the sense of injustice.

Here the main concern is with human dignity. From early times, cruel and unusual punishments have been relegated to the discretion of deity or destiny; law has pulled away from vengeance and humiliation. Vicious and debasing punishments are felt to dishonor the court and the humanity whose authority it wields. Forty stripes were the ancient limit, not so much in the interest of the criminal as of the general respect for man.[7] On the same theory, an alien visitor was considered to be entitled to legal safeguards. In Athens, it was an execrable crime *erranti viam non monstrare*,[8] because the stranger who had lost his way had a residual status as a man.

Human dignity is one of the tacit assumptions of the law.[9] It expresses itself generally in the deep distinctions

---

[7] Deuteronomy 25:3. It was reduced by the rabbis to a maximum of thirty-nine. Tract Maccoth III. VI, in 9 (XVII). Rodkinson, Babylonian Talmud 48 (1918); II Corinthians 11:24.

[8] Cicero, De officiis III. xiii (Loeb's trans. 1928), 323.

[9] The development of Roman tort law may be attributed in substantial part to assimilation of Greek standards of human dignity. *See* Buckland, A Text-Book of Roman Law from Augustus to Justinian 589, *et seq.* (2d ed. 1932); Taubenschlag, The Law of Greco-Roman Egypt in the Light of the Papyri 329, *et seq.* (1944). *Cf.* our own recent discovery of the right of privacy, still inadequately safeguarded.

among accidental, innocent intentional, and guilty intentional conduct. Motives count because man is assumed to be primarily rational, free of will, and capable of choice. When he acts accidentally, he is regarded as the mere instrument of external forces; when he acts intentionally but in good faith, guilt may attach within circumscribed areas: only evil purpose will invoke mortal guilt. No one judges Oedipus as he does Nero, though each intentionally killed a person who was his parent.[10]

Positive law, building upon this dignity, may make it expensive. Thus the ancient Pharisees held that it precluded vicarious responsibility in law, *e.g.*, liability for the wrongful acts of one's slave.[11] And, in our own times, dignity has been held incompatible with requiring collective action in employee relations or prohibiting child labor. The sense of injustice is not so easily taken in: it can penetrate the masquerade.

Instance D. An important patent litigation is pending before an appellate court of three judges. One of them, having received a bribe from the appellant's attorney, succeeds in persuading his honorable colleagues to join with him in deciding for the appellant.

Here we have an example of injustice involved in the operation of the judicial process. The nature of that process requires certain familiar attributes and procedures, such as impartiality, notice, fair hearing, and judgment of defined

---

[10] This reference was lifted baldly from David Hume's An Enquiry Concerning the Principles of Morals (1740), where I thought it originated until, as usual, I found the archetype in Aristotle (Nicomachean Ethics, 1135a).

[11] Finkelstein, The Pharisees 283–85 (1938).

issues predicated upon identifiable evidence. Of course, the judicial process, even when ideally applied, does not lead to ascertainment of all the truth, for there are subliminal values in most disputes which not even the most thorough hearing will disclose. Nor does it lead to judgments of perfect wisdom: the law cannot so individualize its operations as to meet the idiosyncrasy, the irreducible uniqueness of each case. Patterns are developed in the light of the repetitive aspects of litigation, and much that protrudes beyond the pattern must be ignored. But, whatever its pragmatic limitations, the judicial process is required to exhibit a fair effort at finding truth and exercising wisdom. Without that effort — involving notice, hearing, and deliberation — it loses its rank as process; it becomes gross will. Informed by this view, the sense of injustice protests all the more angrily against abuse of legal procedures to serve oppressive or vindictive ends.

Instance E. Some workmen engaged in excavation dig up certain ancient Pythagorean manuscripts and turn them over to the owner of the land. Their contents, hitherto unknown, excite much discussion, which reaches the ears of the city magistrate. He borrows the manuscripts, reads only the table of contents, and determines that the text will have a tendency to undermine established religion. Thereupon the legislature is consulted and, after hearing the magistrate take oath that the books ought not to be read or preserved, decrees that they be publicly burned.[12] This is felt to be unjust.

12 This instance was taken almost literally from Livy XL. 29 (Bohn's trans. 1915), 1885–86.

The concern in this instance is with the authorized functions of government, its right of censorship and relation to freedom of inquiry. There is hardly a conceivable function that government has not arrogated to itself at one time or another, under pretext of divine authority, public welfare, or bald caprice; and judgments of propriety on this score are almost completely relative.[18] Yet censorship of thought somehow remains the most obnoxious of all such interferences, perhaps because it eventually prevents all intelligent amelioration of government itself, perhaps because it insults and degrades the rational claims of the citizen.

What powers men delegate to their governments depend upon what they think of themselves and of their needs. Recognized needs may call for severe abnegation, especially in times of great public emergency. But if the citizenry thinks well of its own intelligence and wisdom, it will bridle at censorship; it will struggle for access to facts and to ideas. Men who do not respect human capacity will raise no such objections. They will feel no loss in being closed out from what they cannot use. Thus, here again the view of law parallels closely the view of human capacities.

Instance F. Relying on a series of formal charters, colonists set out from their homeland and, despite fearful perils and hardships, succeed in building the beginnings of a new pioneer society. They organize local governments and militia, open courts and schools, construct highways, harbors,

18 A negative instance would also have been appropriate; that is, one of the failure of government to fulfill functions that custom or circumstances rendered obligatory. Failure to provide opportunity for productive employment of those able to work might illustrate the case.

and trading centers. Fighting back the savage aborigines, they hew down forests, plough and plant the land, and establish their councils of self-rule. Just at the dawn of their success, the home legislature, thousands of miles away from their new problems and free mores, passes a decree that it has the right to bind the colonies in all cases whatsoever. The sense of injustice is outraged.

In this instance, normal expectations have been disappointed — a species of injustice that embraces many varied actions of legislatures and courts. Any retroactive change in substantive law would, of course, furnish a conspicuous example of such disappointment, for the law itself creates expectation of the consistency and continuity of its own operations. But expectations may arise from other sources, such as the moral views and practices of the community and its economic fabric. The positive law may be unjust in breaking not only its promise of regularity but likewise its promise of adequacy and utility. What is the law good for, if it is deaf to patent needs?

One of these is the need for evolutionary change in the law itself. There is a legitimate expectation that courts and legislatures will discern what is useful and good in new occasions. The sense of injustice may find as much offense in a regularity that is slavish as in an inconsiderate change. In the former case, the provocation generally seems lighter, for the expectation has not been weighted with reliance and the direction of legal progress remains debatable. A prestige of legitimacy attaches to the known law, rebuttable only by showing that it is substantially wrong. At times, there arise revolutionary needs that demand a clean sweep of the established order and will not permit vested rights to stand in the way; but in the usual situation the law can fulfill its function best by seeing that contracts are performed, existing social standards are enforced, and relations which it invited men to create are sustained. Thus it is that judges in moving the law forward, case by case, are always impeded; attitudes and reliances intervene between the precedent and the attempt to improve it. Positive law as it progresses must weigh the utility of the new rule against that of confidence and certainty. The sense of injustice warns against either standing still or leaping forward; it calls for movement in an intelligible design.

What the Instances Show. These instances prick the contours of our topic. The sense of injustice may now be described as a general phenomenon operative in the law. Among its facets are the demands for equality, desert, human dignity, conscientious adjudication, confinement of government to its proper functions, and fulfillment of common expectations. These are facets, not categories. They tend to overlap one another and do not together exhaust the sense of injustice. They should be thought of as facets, each partially shaping the outlines of the others in an almost fluid continuity. They do not resemble a neat row of discrete ice cubes or even the rigid mold that shapes the cubes, for they are only aspects, not parts, of the sense of injustice.

Are these aspects ethical in their nature? They are, for they posit certain explicit values in the realm of human conduct. But they are not merely ethical: as they enter into the shaping of positive law, they acquire a special direction and form qualified by the past history and present felt needs of the juridic system, and modified again by the factor of sanction. An ethical impulse to which legal sanctions have been attached is not quite the same as it was; its content and intensity must shrink to the size of its new responsibility.

Are these aspects of justice universal? Hardly. The claim might be made that they are limits which the variables of positive law tend to approach, and as we presently consider the sources of the sense of injustice that claim may gain some support. It must be remembered, however, that most of these aspects pertain to the operation of law rather than to its substance, and that positive rules contribute a great deal to the body and meaning of equality, legitimacy of expectations, and so forth. The universal element would thus appear exceedingly narrow, and may be restricted to inescapable natural dimensions such as the integral status of individual man.

Concepts may be real without being universal. In any sound pragmatic sense, principles are real so far as they have meaningful consequences. Of course, their rank may be made to vary with their universality, but loftiness of rank is all too often achieved by means of dilution and excessive thinning. Our interest here is rather in the real qua efficacious. Utterly universal operation of one cause would crowd out all others; it would destroy the dynamism of nature and level human life to monotony. Insistence on perfect universality would lead only to an ultimate colorless abstraction " sans everything." In the finite world of which we speak, the genuinely efficient causes are finite and plural; finite effects suggest and indicate finite causes. The justice that we can learn to know is neither completely universal nor categorically right; by that token, it is real in human affairs. It makes a practical difference.

Nor need we view the sense of injustice as dangling beneath some hypostatic framework of natural law, itself suspended from divine law in a chain of infinite regress. The law of nature may exist, may not exist, or may linger in the limbo of doubt for purposes of this inquiry, whose movement is forward to consequences, not backward to origins. We are concerned with studying the sense of injustice, not as a product or effect, but as an operative cause in the law. Thus it is that Ockham's razor excises natural law from our present interest; it does not excise the sense of injustice unless all the phenomena of positive law could be explained without it.

Finally, the sense of injustice is no mere generic label for the concepts already reviewed. It denotes that sympathetic reaction of outrage, horror, shock, resentment, and anger, those affections of the viscera and abnormal secretions of the adrenals that prepare the human animal to resist attack. Nature has thus equipped all men to regard injustice to another as personal aggression. Through a mysterious and magical *empathy* or imaginative interchange, each projects himself into the shoes of the other, not in pity or compassion merely, but in the vigor of self-defense. Injustice is transmuted into assault; the sense of injustice is the implement by which assault is discerned and defense is prepared.

Justice thus acquires its public meaning, as those in a given ethos perceive the same threat and experience the same organic reactions. It is possible to speak of justice without utter relativism or solipsism, just because of this astonishing interchangeability within man's imagination. If a man did not have the capacity to recognize oppression of another as a species of attack upon himself, he would be unready — in the glandular sense — to face the requirements of juridic survival. In fine, the human animal is predisposed to fight injustice.

This predisposition like other natural capacities is designed to end in action. The individual man stands at the center of all things, bound by the perspective predicament to his own brief time and narrow place. The sense of injustice gives him a lengthening tether so that he may wander away from self and its setting. But tethered he remains. His survival does not require that the sense of injustice encompass infinitude; at a certain distance from the center in sympathy and circumstance, his reaction will shade off into contemplation, cool appraisal, and ultimate indifference. There are wrongs that retain only literary concernment. Iphigenia and her sorrows are such an instance.

Our awareness, however, is not necessarily lulled by mere disparity of culture, law, or ethical tradition, for Socrates' fate haunts the thoughts of every generation. The criterion is whether the circumstances permit imaginative interchange. If the specific threat be such as to project itself out of history and into the radius of possible experience, it becomes real, it calls for action. For example, corrupt judges and mob passion are ominous in every age.

The experience of the sense of injustice is of a social nature, enlarging the calculus of individual chances. What may or may not affect the particular human being in his own small ambit will inevitably, in the course of sufficient time, touch someone somewhere. That is why the jural status of each is felt to depend upon a just order of increasingly wide extension.

The sense of injustice now appears as an indissociable blend of reason and empathy. It is evolutionary in its manifestations. Without reason, it could not serve the ends of social utility, which only observation, analysis, and science can discern. Without empathy, it would lose its warm sensibility and its cogent natural drive. It is compounded, indissolubly, of both and can subsist on neither alone. For sheer rationality without an empathic fundament would usually degenerate to extreme skepticism and doubt; while empathy, uninformed by reason, would serve up only the illiterate gropings of animal faith. Together reason and empathy support our juridic world. Through them men may learn to identify their own interests with those of an unlimited community, no longer doubting in philosophy what they do not doubt in their hearts.[14]

Is the sense of injustice right? Certainly not, if rightness means conformity to some absolute and inflexible standard. There is nothing so easy or mechanical about it. Blended as it is of empathy and reason, its correctness in particular cases will vary greatly, for how can we know that the intellect has understood and that projection has comprehended every last relevant factor? Who will measure the limits of inquiry or affix the seal of completeness?

Fortunately we appear able to dispense with such a seal, accepting in its stead the assurances that come from inner conviction and from juridic experience. The sense of injustice is right in so far as its claims are recognized in ac-

---

[14] A paraphrase of two unrelated sentences of C. S. Peirce. The Philosophy of Peirce 163, 229 (Buchler ed. 1940).

tion. Its logical justification must be found in its efficacy, for it succeeds in fact precisely to the extent that relevant circumstances have been understood, felt, and appreciated. Like other biological equipment it endures because it serves, and serves better through progressive adaptation. So, despite all blunders and insensibilities, the sense of injustice is on the right side, the side of fallible men. Offering a common language for communication and mutual defense, it reduces the perils of isolation. It affords some warrant of a progressively better legal order, and thus makes law a vehicle of persuasion. Plato has said that the creation of the world is the victory of persuasion over force; [15] the instrument of that victory is justice.

III. *Justice in Positive Law*

If the drafts already drawn in the course of this study have been honored by the reader, credit has been extended on two attractive grounds. In the first place, the sense of injustice presupposes all the richness and diversity of experience, and all the skills that develop with an accruing wisdom. Part of this experience is emotional, a circumstance that lends intimacy and human warmth to the whole. Part is rational, permitting growth, progression, and cumulation. Together these demonstrate themselves in consciousness and memory; they are known because they are felt. Hence the exposition has derived from very familiar data which it is difficult not to trust.

Moreover, the sense of injustice has been kept in its

[15] Using Dr. Whitehead's summary of various sentiments in the Timaeus (particularly at 48A). Whitehead, Adventures of Ideas 105 (1937). *See also* Laws IV, 718B–723D (Loeb's trans. 1926), 300–18.

place. We have not forgotten that the Romans often appointed a dictator simply to drive a nail into the temple wall [16] or that heriots continued until this generation in English property tenure.[17] While insisting that justice is significant in the compound of the law, we have not been so blind as to treat the two as interchangeable. There are great realms of justice outside of positive law; there are wide areas of positive law where justice is of weak or indifferent influence. But as justice without law is often ineffectual, law without justice is quite unthinkable. A system of utterly unjust law could exist in the imagination only and could serve none but casuistic purposes.

Now, of course, many wrongs have been committed in the name of justice. It has received much hypocritical lip service and has furnished a convenient motto for fools and rascals. The positive effectuality of the sense of injustice can hardly be established by quoting judicial protestation, however eloquent. The evidence needed here must be more empirically convincing. If the sense of injustice is a real causal factor in the daily operation of law, the area of its consequences must be marked out, for that is where its validity and meaning will reside. The consequences may be taken either at random, illustrating the scope of the causation, or systematically, indicating its pervasiveness.

For example, the aspect of equality shows itself in the

[16] Livy VII. 3, VIII. 18 (Bohn's trans. 1889), 450, 528. The custom was supposed to have stemmed "from the memory of the more aged, that a pestilence had formerly been relieved, on the nail being driven by a dictator." *Cf.* Frazer, The Golden Bough 44, 127 (1 vol. ed. 1937).

[17] The heriot was the lord's archaic right to seize the best beast or other chattel of a deceased tenant. It was adjusted and disposed of by the Law of Property Act, 1922, 12 & 13 Geo. V, c. 16, § 140. In New England, heriots had been prohibited by Article 10 of the Body of Liberties adopted by the General Court of Massachusetts in 1641.

proposition that no human being, however exalted, may lawfully cause the death of an unoffending neighbor, however insignificant, even to save his own life.[18] By like token, where indictment or trial calls for the judgment of equal citizens, a procedure that violates equality will be unlawful and void.[19] The status in jeopardy is prime, that is to say, not reducible. The implications of this status may be extended, so that life comprehends livelihood: thus discrimination by labor unions [20] or employers [21] as between human integers may be prohibited in positive law. It is because new valuable equalities are constantly being uncovered that the term acquires meaning and rises above forensic incantation.

Random Instances. Without further multiplication of

[18] Dudley, Stephens, and Brooks, three seamen, and a boy named Richard Parker were the crew of an English yacht which was caught in a storm 1,600 miles from the Cape of Good Hope. They took to an open boat together. As they drifted on the ocean, their meager supply of food, including a turtle which they caught, lasted barely twelve days. By the twentieth day, all of them were in a state of extreme weakness and prostration. There was still no sail in sight nor any other prospect of relief. And so, with the approval of Stephens but not of Brooks, Dudley dragged himself over to where Richard Parker lay and stuck a knife into the throat of the helpless boy. The three men fed on the body for four days. On the fourth day, they were picked up by a passing vessel. Dudley and Stephens were tried and both were held guilty of murder. Queen v. Dudley, 14 Q. B. D. 273 (1884). A similarly colorful instance is United States v. Holmes, 26 Fed. Cas. 360 No. 15,383 (C. C. E. D. Pa. 1842). As Rabha said: " Rather than slay another, thou must permit thyself to be slain; for how dost thou know that thy blood is better than his, perchance his blood is better than thine? " — Tract Pesachim, c. II, in 3 (V) Rodkinson, Babylonian Talmud 37 (1918).

[19] For example, the exclusion of members of the defendant's race from the grand jury or trial jury.

[20] In Steele v. Louisville & N. R. R., 323 U. S. 192 (1944), the Supreme Court held that a labor union, which under the provisions of a statute acted as collective bargaining representative of workers in a certain craft, could not legally enter into an agreement that discriminated against Negro workers in that craft.

[21] Fair employment practices commissions have been among the positive gains realized during the Second World War. *See also* Art. 123 of the constitution of the U.S.S.R.

examples, mention of one or two striking instances of positive justice may illustrate sufficiently its lively inventiveness. The first of these relating to the aspect of desert presented an occasion of great international moment. At the end of the European phase of the Second World War, the sense of injustice everywhere called for the punishment of those who had committed wholesale wrongs in preparation or conduct of war. " The feeling of outrage grew in this country, and it became more and more felt that these were crimes committed against us and against the whole society of civilized nations by a band of brigands who had seized the instrumentality of a state." Confessedly lacking any satisfactorily clear precedent, the positive law had here either to innovate or to confess its impotence. It innovated, holding that the " test of what legally is crime gives recognition to those things which fundamentally outraged the conscience of the American people and brought them finally to the conviction that their own liberty and civilization could not persist in the same world with the Nazi power." [22] It would be supererogatory to comment that these phrases coincide with our description of the sense of injustice, its perception of wrong as a species of attack, and its marshaling of organic defense. Desert could be satisfied though precedent, statute, and convention were at best ambiguous.

Another stimulating instance is afforded in *Bridges v. Wixon* [23] where new light was cast upon the aspect of hu-

[22] The quotations are from the epochal report of Justice Robert H. Jackson as Chief of Counsel for the United States. Trial of War Criminals (Dept. of State No. 2420) 5, 7 (1945).

[23] This was an attempt to deport Harry Bridges, an alien who entered the United States in 1920 and became an important labor leader. The statute directed exclusion or deportation of aliens who were members of or

man dignity. In the *Bridges* litigation, the Supreme Court considerably narrowed the proposition that legally serious guilt can be acquired by mere association. Since human beings are unique and individual entities, each may claim to be tried and judged on his own acts and pronouncements, severed from those of all others. This is merely the legal facet of a millennial dilemma in morals, for at the same time each human being is also a cell in the social organism and in the complex tissue of its members, operating always as a socius with others, never through himself alone. Qua citizen, his capacity to act at all is a social power, drawn from affiliation. Thus he is simultaneously all selfness and all otherness. The graph of his legal duties and responsibilities is no simple one; in the *Bridges* case, the decision could not properly have followed either axis of reference without regard to the other. Bridges was neither a monad in isolation, answerable for itself alone, nor a fungible portion of some organization, equivalent to any other portion. Human dignity could be respected only by regarding him to some extent as both. Such was the Court's view: he was held not guilty by association, because the evidence of association was too flimsy and tenuous; but the majority of the justices would not exclude vicarious liability as such.

The sense of injustice is thus an active, spontaneous source of law, contributing its current to the juridic stream. It makes a practical working difference in legislatures, courts, and administrative bodies. Justice is useful

affiliated with any organization advocating overthrow of the government by force. The evidence offered in order to prove Bridges' affiliation with the Communist party was held insufficient. Bridges v. Wixon, 326 U. S. 135 (1945).

to society, for the reason, among others, that it gives men a sense of physical and psychic security. Every positive act of justice represents not only the absence of attack but the bulwarking of habits, techniques, and standards which safeguard against attacks to come. This is a prime social beneficence. It furthers solidarity at the very seat of all centripetal impulses — the imaginations of men. We need not therefore rest content with a shallow utilitarianism, nor assert that the useful is the just, that law is just only because it is socially useful. Justice has a nobler claim to regard. The law becomes useful in being just, for justice creates and confers utility. Justice is a source not a mere by-product of the useful; injustice, by like token, is pragmatically unwise and wasteful.

Now this is not to say that law is predetermined to move ever closer toward relations which would satisfy the demands of the sense of injustice. There may be such a tropism, but in the available conspectus (legal history being relatively quite brief) it certainly appears irregular and spasmodic. The sense of injustice calls for progressive exhibition of human wisdom. Hence until some demonstration can be made of accumulation, not to say evolution, in that respect, the movement of law toward justice will remain a matter of faith and resolution, rather than of scientific fact. What matters most for the practical concerns of men is that injustice be prevented or rectified in the particular case or group of cases.

Justice and the Analytical Approach. A systematic view of justice in positive law would require something more than the very vital but nonetheless random instances considered above. Its approach might be analytic or insti-

tutional. The analytic approach is addressed to the implements of legal process, for example, rules of law, and seeks
to illumine the interplay between them on the one hand
and justice on the other.

Rules are one of law's attributes. The legal evaluation
of any set of circumstances depends upon the application of
a considerable body of rules. Often this application is el-
liptic, for lawyers and judges tacitly assume the axioms of
the law and its established propositions. A cumulative network of precedent and corollary may lie behind the sim-
plest determination. The process is an indispensable one,
given the limitations of judges in intellect and wisdom, the
brevity of human life, the repetitiveness of transactions,
and the necessity of planning for the future. Rules are
the charts of the law, by their very existence keeping most
affairs out of the courts and conferring safety and meaning upon the relations of men. Through summation of
past dispositions as the current law, rules create psychological values of belief, faith, and security; but it must be
conceded that they frequently fail as guides to the outcome
of particular incipient cases. They are better histories
than prophecies. Men being the believing and conserva-
tive creatures that they are find legal history, if sufficiently
recent, an adequate assurance of tomorrow's decision; men
being the venturesome creatures that they are generally accept the risks involved.

The rule, viewed in utilitarian terms, is an implement of
economy. It lifts the burdens of judges and reduces the
unknowns for litigants and for those who wish to avoid
becoming litigants. In terms of a more ambitious analysis, the rule is an embodiment of the principle of equality.

It furnishes the juridic machinery by which equal situations are equally adjudged. Thus legal propositions represent something more than a technique of useful regularity; they serve to fulfill one of the functions of concrete justice.

But here again an antinomy arises, of twofold nature: an antinomy within regularity and within justice, each functionally related to the other.

The antinomy within regularity is an all too familiar one. Without assuming that a judge's decision follows simply from his childhood fixations or his basal metabolism (a shallow type of cynicism), we must grant that rules do not decide cases. Literature and experience to this effect are too voluminous for detailed recapitulation here. Cases there may be in which the aleatory element is infinitesimal, but they are relatively few and their outlines are simple; that is to say, not simple but simplified, for the rule may be preserved in operation by a ruthless refusal to consider available differentiae. Simplicity in law facts is not given by experience but achieved by means of exclusion.

For the generality of litigation, much depends upon choice of facts on the one hand and choice of rules on the other. Since testimony and documents are susceptible of various appreciations, the judge and jury are free within astonishingly wide limits to choose their facts. And as rules of law, particularly in cognate fields (*e.g.*, contract and tort), compete with one another to control the disposition of the case, reaching the decision may well involve a choice of rule. This explains that not infrequent phenomenon: a decision based on a ground which neither side had briefed. Of course, the choices are not unrelated, for facts are found with a view to the ultimate application of some legal rule. Thus, the combined choices make up an appreciation of the whole controversy; and as this appreciation is the complex performance of mortal minds, it must remain contingent, at least partly free, hence at least partly unpredictable. But, then, what of the security that the rules of law were supposed to confer?

There is likewise an antinomy within justice, pertaining to the system of rules. We noted above that legal principles serve certain valuable functions of justice, such as equality and the fulfillment of legitimate expectations. This much is true, but it is also true that rules of law may be unjust, unequal, and oppressive. Justice in a particular class of cases may collide head on with the established rule. Rules at best are like windows over the landscape; at some line or other they must excise the balance of the scene, perhaps its most significant part. At worst the rule may operate as an impenetrable blind, closing out all perception of the actualities of the case. On the other hand, to avoid the rule is apparently equivalent to denial of justice, for legitimate expectations will be frustrated. When rules, the supposed emanation of justice, absorb the reverence that is rightfully due to their source alone (a process all too familiar in theology), how can the dilemma be resolved?

Perhaps both of these antinomies arise out of a fallacious belief that rules are the law. Legal rules of a synthetic nature, that is, those which limit and define the rights and duties of men and the procedures by which they are enforced, are not the law, but its instruments. We say, by way of ellipsis, that the law is changed when a rule of law has been changed; such an identification of the institution with one type of its working tools generally does no harm. But the contradictions which we have just considered show that the ellipsis may lead to an impasse in theory. The implement appears to conflict with the very purpose it was designed to effectuate. This is because the function of the implement has been misunderstood.

Rules are indeed implements of justice in law, but not of justice alone. We have said that justice is only one element in the legal compound, amalgamated there with a variety of other human interests, some lofty enough, some rather earthy. Through the machinery of rules, each of these impulses seeks maximum satisfaction. The rules change and accommodate themselves not merely with the flux and movement of historic forces but with new and subtle equilibria among these interests. Thus the sense of injustice may outweigh a professional desire for symmetry, or may itself yield, at least temporarily, to the bulk of some economic demand — whose validity it will adjudge sooner or later. All these motions are conveyed into legal action through the conduit of rules. Out of their interplay arise the presuppositions and conceptual jargon of lawyers and judges.

This is not to say that justice is no more valuable to law than, for example, the desire of courts to rationalize their decisions. It is first and most potent. The many other interests which combine to form what we call law turn to justice for their sanction and draw from it their more enduring strength. Men in the mass are never long content to shrug their shoulders and sigh " *dura lex sed lex* "; security in human affairs is one of law's most vigorous impulses, but it cannot be held forever at the cost of justice.

As Aristotle pointed out, justice in the general sense embraces all the other virtues; though we speak of it here in the particular (juridic) sense, its status as theoretic gravamen of the others remains. Justice is to security and legal logic as bedrock to the foundations and flying buttresses of a cathedral. Thus in the appreciation and choice of fact and controlling law, the sense of injustice is a dependable criterion, though concededly not the exclusive one. Justice is what judges and juries try to serve, despite the narrow channels which have been dug for them and their own all too human frailties. So limited, they generally do what they can to select facts and law toward a conceivedly just result. In the process, the rule of law may be slowly transmuted, perhaps by using the familiar techniques of distinction, legal presumption, or exclusion from evidence. The sense of injustice thus assists propositions of law to find their application in particular cases, while it expands or erodes the propositions themselves. For law is an institution whose action in human affairs necessarily involves its own evolution. The only static law is inoperative law.

In the reign of Henry II, proceedings on the writ of right for recovery of land resulted in intolerable delays, some on dilatory pretexts of poor health or the King's business, others on successive vouchers to warranty.[24] Now the granting of these delays was the established rule, derived from obvious principles of fairness; for a sick man could not be expected to fight a trial by combat and an owner whose title was challenged should certainly be en-

[24] I follow here Jenks's somewhat simplified narrative. Short History of English Law 49–50 (5th ed. 1938). A slightly different emphasis is given in 2 Pollock and Maitland, History of English Law 44–49 (1895). *See also* Plucknett, A Concise History of the Common Law 321 (1940).

abled to bring in his vendor. But ill-health might linger, the defendant's vendor might vouch his vendor to warranty, and the champing plaintiff was not immortal. Meanwhile the land he claimed was held by another; he had paper instead of soil. The sense of injustice — here in relation to the judicial process — came into play and transformed the rules. That the Crown needed to ascertain precisely where the title stood and thus where liability lay for military service and for taxes may have expedited the solution, but could not alone account for its later dignity and permanence. The justices invented an appropriate proceeding. They conducted a simple inquest to decide who had the latest anterior possession and then they awarded interim possession accordingly.[25] The *status quo* was restored, provisionally but effectually. The provisional gradually became the permanent, as the expense and delay involved in trying paper title became detached from the practical advantages of possession. Thus possession or seisin eventually acquired that fundamental role in the common law which it still enjoys. The sense of injustice had, perhaps in collaboration with other impulses, changed the rule of law and called a new juridic institution into being.

In this manner the Ought of law goes far to determine the Is; the forms and functions of legal norms vary with their ends. Of course, it is not always within the power of courts to mold propositions to the felt needs of the community. The task may be such that only a statute will suffice. Creation or restoration of a fitting proportionate-

---

[25] Referring to the assizes of mort d'ancestor, novel disseisin, and d'arrein presentment.

ness among various economic groups is usually a matter for the legislature. But the considerations involved remain much the same, and the sense of injustice may be as assertive and evocative in one place as the other. Legislators may indeed satisfy it more freely. They feel less trammeled by professional inhibitions, and may amputate where judges could only dose. Their errors like the courts' can generally be attributed to inadequate appreciation of relevant factors, inadequate sympathetic interchange, or both. The sense of injustice, however, is never quite dormant in positive lawmaking. It joins the expectation of regularity to a coequal expectation of progression, and demands that both of them be satisfied in the same process.

Justice and the Institutions of Law. If the implements of law respond to impulses of justice, so too do its institutions. Out of all the sprawling paraphernalia of the law, taxation would probably afford the most persuasive example. As tax measures appear to stem so completely from sheer command or sovereign will, whatever traces of justice they may evince will augur well for other legal institutions. Of course, even should the quest of justice in taxation prove successful, it could not amount to a general and absolute demonstration. Our analysis is one of open ends, which requires us to forego certain charming correspondences; what is true, however, of taxation should apply a fortiori to almost all portions of the law. The combined facet of equality-desert will be described as it shows itself in tax law, leaving the play of other aspects of justice to cursory mention.

Tax systems of modern nations exhibit superficially such profuse variety as to challenge the very possibility of general statement. They do however deal with much the same factual matrix — human beings and their relations to economic goods; and for that very reason the respective systems do resemble one another in many basic respects. A rough pattern can be formed out of the similarities, showing the major outline of taxation but virtually none of its domestic detail.

For example, each individual person has with respect to taxation a dual status. As citizen or inhabitant he is a tax unit, and as bearer of relations to economic goods he is also a tax unit. The former status is an integral one and imports the sort of elementary equality among individuals that obtains in respect to their civil rights. It is expressed not quite perfectly in such devices as the poll tax, general sales tax, or the Soviet turnover tax. In time of national emergency or war, as the civil status of the individual becomes his most critical attribute, these types of tax acquire a special justification. In a more normal economy, however, their importance tends to recede, not merely in the light of practical fiscal considerations, but also because economic status then outweighs the civil in an individual's relations to government.

The equality applicable to economic status is expressed familiarly in the principle of ability to pay. Economic status is highly differentiable — *e.g.*, as regards capital, income, mode of doing business, family grouping, mode of gratuitous transfer or receipt; and the adaptation of ability to pay to these and other differentiae is indeed a long and winding story. For the present analysis, the motif alone will suffice. Through progressive taxation of economic relations, governments apply that proportionateness which Aristotle found the true substance of justice.[26] The equality here is that of an ascending rate series. Those equally situated in relation to economic goods are taxed approximately the same, and strenuous efforts are exerted to protect the equality against avoidance schemes and factitious distinctions. Of course, this policy becomes intense wherever taxation is employed not only to raise revenue but also to reduce economic inequalities.

Patently, not all tax systems conform as they should to these criteria of equality. Nevertheless, while awaiting the millennium, we are justified in taking note of an imperfect and variable equality which seems to mark the current state of human affairs. Its realness, visible in a multitude of observable consequences, will be doubted only by those who insist on all or nothing. But even they may concede that here again the just confers utility, for ability to pay demonstrably brings in the revenues.

Human dignity in taxation is expressed quite generally in subsistence exemptions and in various techniques of self-assessment. Justice in the functions of government may show itself, affirmatively, through use of taxation to destroy or reduce deleterious practices and conditions, or, negatively, through exemption of religious practices and communication of thought. Disappointment of legitimate expectations may be avoided by denying retrospective application to tax statutes. Thus the various facets of justice radiate quite clearly even in the grubby business of collecting taxes. In other fields of law, their light and influence should be at least equally manifest.

[26] Nicomachean Ethics, 1131a, in The Basic Works of Aristotle 1010 (McKeon ed. 1941). Aristotle was probably the first to explicate the use of taxation for regulatory purposes. Politics, 1309a, *id.* at 1248.

Justice in positive law is a profuse theme. Random instances, limited analysis of legal implements, and comments upon one particular institution cannot begin to explicate all its vital diversity. The little that has been said may serve to reduce cynicism and to vindicate the sense of injustice as an active maker and shaper of law. It works on a grand scale and within the narrow interstices of procedure. The justice we were looking for was not in the ether, but in the courts and legislatures and in the transactions of men.

IV. *Power and Justice*

The Limits of Power. At the opposite pole of the antinomy is the concept of power, the ability to cause, modify, or arrest motion. Patently, the power of the sovereign is only one species of this kinetic capacity, for human beings are affected by many such influences, inanimate or animate, adventitious or teleological. Floods and droughts have power to change the course of men's conduct, and so too have parents, wives and children, partners and friends, superstitions and syllogisms. Some of these may effect deeper and more lasting motion than any decree or secret police force. They can penetrate farther into the imaginations of men, which are the primary reservoirs of all social power, including that of the sovereign.

Now it is naïve to speak of sovereign power without differentiation. Exercise exhausts some powers; to others it brings an increase of information and skill. Degeneration of the sovereign and stupid arrogance have often followed from an excess of power. The speed and judgment exhibited by the government are seen to slacken in accordance with a law of marginal efficacy; and the subjects when pressed too hard may progressively deteriorate as regards zeal or understanding. The power concept is not a simple one. Yet it has gained an uncritical credulity from those who are most skeptical of justice. Absolute reason having shown feet of clay, the disillusioned idealist builds a shrine to absolute caprice. He identifies law with command. But will is not made rational by being rationalized; without reason it remains chaotic as reason without will becomes impotent.

Sovereign power has its competitors in human imagination and its limits in pragmatic effectiveness. Citizens can always die rather than obey, and history shows in ample detail that they do. Sometimes they do not die alone, and their willingness to die may have a special power of its own. In any event, as a matter of sheer common sense, the sovereign's capacity to kill those who stand in his way is not tantamount to having his way, for corpses make very poor subjects. The most ruthless of tyrants cannot create expedient deeds out of the nihilism of his will. If he wishes order to further his arbitrary purposes, he must be somewhat orderly himself; there must be method in his willfulness.

Thus it is that the net of regularity entangles not only justice but also power. Exertions of power through the medium of law must apply to rather definite categories of human affairs, to transactions that repeat themselves and by repetition beat out discernible paths. These categories are constitutive to legal power; they prescribe the routes it may travel and the ends it may seek. If law were only sovereign command, it would nevertheless remain a command uttered in the chambers of the given cosmos, with its predeterminations, its habits and heavy inertia.

This despot to whom we referred would find himself restrained by all the competitive motivations of his subjects (ranging from religious conviction to gluttony) and all the trammels of governmental organization (ranging from party intrigues to shortage of carbon paper). He must give his commands to lawyers and judges, subordinating his pure will to all the meshes of semantics. And, worst of all, the men of the law have their established professional habits.[27] Perhaps among them there is a Coke, Papinian, or Thomas More. If not, the frustrations still continue, for lawyers will doggedly proceed by deliberation, by ratiocination, however weak, and by some species of formalized process. The most venal of them, striving to please him, may construe his decrees too narrowly or too broadly, for he cannot enslave the language in which he speaks. But if the judges are men, they will discover a multitude of fretful ways to cross and defeat his purposes.

Is it then permissible to say that law is mere sovereign will? Not in any sound empirical sense. The statement is moreover hopelessly inadequate, for it explains so little. A will with force behind it can hardly coincide with law — every highwayman wields that kind of authority. Will

[27] Article 418 of the Civil Code of the Russian Socialist Federated Soviet Republic limits freedom of testamentary disposition by specifying restricted classes of permissible beneficiaries. New York's Decedent Estate Law, Consolidated Laws of New York, c. 13, § 18, limits the same freedom by requiring certain minimum provisions for the surviving spouse. It seems no mere coincidence that these statutes were construed by the respective courts not to apply to gratuitous dispositions *inter vivos*. Supreme Court R. S. F. S. R. July 9, 1923, pr. No. 12; Newman v. Dore, 275 N. Y. 371, 9 N. E. (2d) 966 (1937).

and force do not sufficiently restrict the possibilities of the conception. They do not begin to answer the question: What is the sovereign to will?

Is he to will only the increase of his own power? The hypothesis is that it cannot be increased, for it is presumed to be as absolute as possible. Perhaps he should will its continuance. Well, then, he must find ways to introduce efficiency and dependability, a scheme of order in his great household. His service comes from men; their bodies must be preserved, their loyalty enlisted, and their minds conditioned. He will not wish to be caught in the trap of his people's witlessness.

Some few statutes in a typical legal system may relate to the continuance of governmental power; *e.g.*, punishments for interfering with policemen in the performance of their duties or measures of censorship. But most of the grand body of legislation in any country discloses no such direct purpose. It seeks rather to effectuate all those subtle and complex impulses, sensible and archaic, interested and altruistic, which together comprise the law. It responds to millions of large and petty sovereigns, for every holder of mind, muscle, skill, or property is *pro tanto* a sovereign, capable of enforcing his will upon others through juridic means.

It has long been fashionable to scoff at the myth of social compact, but here we have wandered amid the unrealities of an even less credible fantasy. Law is not whatever the sovereign commands. Sovereign power is finite, keeling over whenever the wind in its sails proves too much for the ballast in its hold. It can effect much in the formulation of the social order; how much depends upon the appeal made to the human sources of its efficacy and on the existing forms of positive law.

As state power goes to the making and modification of law, so also law creates and shapes the power of the state. It prescribes the channels through which energies may flow and its institutions stand to block or divert the stream. Law is not merely a logical antecedent to the authority of the sovereign; it reacts with and upon that authority. Even overthrow of the government does not necessarily end a mature system of positive law. Revolutionaries may change the given positive law in one or many respects, but a substantial residue will persist, including all the practices and tacit standards that serve as the hypothesis of the whole structure. It seems, at any rate, that the Soviet Revolution, which is the most profound of modern times, has done more to change the political map of Europe than to recast the customary values of the Russian people. Some social and legal institutions can be erased by mass convulsions, but others are apparently as indelible as the contours of a seacoast; they change at a geologic pace.

A Pattern of Progress. The authority of the state, finite as we have found it, follows an evolutionary pattern, which, though by no means a necessary résumé of the life of any particular sovereignty, sums up the progression of state power in general. The pattern we are about to describe is not a historical formula, but a scheme of biologic growth. Moreover, the highest observable stage of that growth does not guarantee the survival of a state any more than the evolutionary excellence of the human being can exempt him from the venom of snakes or the infection of tsetse flies. Evolution, of course, looks rather to the fitness

of the whole species, which may nevertheless survive or
succumb because of extraneous causes. In the case of national states, survival may depend upon natural resources,
inventions, fortunate emergence of foresighted leaders, traditional alliances, population, and climate. All of these
factors may obscure but do not invalidate the pattern of
evolutionary ascent.

The lowest level of state power is that which requires
continuous application of force; for example, the power of
a conquering army. On this level, authority is limited not
only by the range of available weapons, but also by the
feasibility of using them without destroying the value of
the conquest. The occupying troops can make and apply
rules of law, but these rules will of necessity relate only
to most primitive concerns — order, food, fuel, quarters.
This is power *in invitum*.

The next level may be called submissional power, for it
is characterized by the passiveness of the population. This
is the stage attained by a despotic polity, whether in relation to the home country or to its colonies. Legal rules
may embrace wide areas of human activity, but coming as
they do from an alien and intellectually distant source they
often fail to reflect the customs and transactional modes of
the people. Thus two bodies of law may exist side by
side, one resorted to by castes favored by the sovereign,
the other inconspicuously but effectually enforced in popular forums. Submissional power is exceedingly friable;
e.g., when Hannibal invaded Italy, the commons in almost
every Italian town rallied to his aid.

But when he had reached the gates of Rome, the mer-
chants in the city showed their defiance by buying up the

very land on which his army was encamped. The power of such a state is consensual. Its government possesses the consent of the governed. This consent need not imply democratic or representative techniques, for authoritarian regimes have frequently enjoyed just such support. Here the legal system attains completeness, emanating as it does from a conceivedly legitimate source. Delegation of power may be explicit in some instances, implied and accepted in others. What counts is that the legislators, elective or hereditary, have constitutional competence.

The consensual stage is the highest attainable for those portions of positive law which laymen would call "technical." Just as state power is confided to the organs of sovereignty, so the organization and maintenance of the legal structure must be assigned to lawyers. For example, the distinction between vested and contingent remainders cannot be determined by popular ballot or by royal lineage. Though a statute or decree may be needed to untie the knot, it will be a professional solution to a professional dilemma. Lawyers, understandably enough, like to embrace all areas of law in this kind of procuration, as long as laymen rest content to have them do so. The consequences are obvious: justice is too often subordinated to the positive, progress to regularity.

State power is susceptible of still further evolution — to the assensual level. At this level, authority is exercised with the active concurrence of the governed. They participate in the formulation and weighing of measures, they influence the movement of the law. This is the stage of the enlightened and alert electorate, of vocal public opinion informed and deliberate. It is compatible with and even beneficial to representative government, lifting the quality of delegates, holding them to account, drawing out their best. At the assensual level, major decisions concerning positive law express the considered opinion of the citizenry, the values and standards for which it is willing to answer. Hence it is that power turns destructively on itself whenever it chokes inquiry and the free play of thought.

Only at this high level is the synthesis possible between justice and power. As the force of the state rises from brutality to consent and ultimately to intelligent assent, it finally attains the same heights as the sense of injustice itself; for the perception of social wrong and the impulse to cure it is a great and potent force. At times, it has proved irresistible.

The sense of injustice does not, however, await this ideal synthesis, the slow triumph of assensual power. On the contrary, it works aggressively toward that consummation. On every level of sovereignty, from the basest to the highest, it influences the thoughts and acts of human beings; even tyrants and their judges cannot make themselves insensible, for they too are men. When they offend, it is the sense of injustice that is offended, and the awareness of the offense is a prime evolutionary impetus. Once an action is felt to be sanctioned by power alone, the doer becomes less powerful, while action by grace of justice gains in strength. The sense of injustice escorts and admonishes the state on its long road toward assensual power.

Justice and power, then, are both deeply real to law, and both are finite. These truths present the first challenge of an anthropocentric jurisprudence: to harness power to social purpose, to refine and develop positive concepts that they may prefigure a worthier commonwealth. " Law exists for men between whom there is injustice." [28]

[28] Nicomachean Ethics, 1134a, in The Basic Works of Aristotle 1012 (McKeon ed. 1941).

FREEDOM AND ORDER

Freedom, n. *Exemption from the stress of authority in a beggarly half dozen of restraint's
infinite multitude of methods.*
> —BIERCE, *The Devil's Dictionary*

I. *The Elements*

THAT MEN, subject incessantly as they are to hunger,
disease, and fear, should ever have conceived of freedom is a great wonder. The commodity is quite scarce in
human experience; yet it has had a variety of formulations
in the history of thought. All of these were affected, like
our own ideas, by the influences of time and place; all were
shots at the infinite released from a finite bow. But the
shots have been aimed in relatively few directions, and their
trajectories at least are instructive. A jurisprudence of
freedom must take the most imposing of them into account.

The oldest and loftiest notion of freedom is presented by
contemplative philosophy. It teaches that men may be
emancipated from insatiable ambition, the play of chance,
and the tyranny of the testes, if only they will repudiate
the values of the world and their own relentless drives.
They may learn to look upon the human scene as neither
comedy nor tragedy, but the way the gods regard it, as a
passing show. This requires a rather complete exemption
from labor and affection, from possessions, and perhaps
even from compassion. It involves a resolute withdrawal
from the arena of affairs, sometimes accompanied by a

touch of contempt for those who remain.[1] In jurisprudence, it fits well with a positivist or formalist attempt to avoid the study of values; for the struggle to discover the just and the practicable and to establish them in the law calls for unusual hardihood. In any event, we cannot all remove to Olympus, and if we did we should have to face the problems of social life there.

The romantic school came somewhat closer to the meaning of freedom, but failed to perceive how it might be made real. Break the barriers, they said, tear down established restraints and inconvenient institutions, and men will be free. Freedom consists in the absence of restraint. But all this meant, when translated into statutes and decisions, was *laissez faire, laissez exploiter*. Without legal restraint, men became free to devour one another. Continued striving — Goethe's ideal — can bring about conditions of continual strife. Hence whether romanticism was formulated in terms of natural law or found its expression in constitutional bills of rights, it offered no lasting guide. It had failed to recognize that neighbors are the chief factor in men's environment.

The statists, including Hegelian and Marxian schools, have found little else to recognize. Whether their approach be economic, dialectic, or political, all here agree that freedom is predominantly an attribute of the social organism and only derivatively of the human cells in it. It is society's function, exercised through the state, to make men free at whatever cost, even the cost of what seem to be

---

[1] The specifically American manifestation of this spirit has been aptly called "Desperate Naturalism." Schneider, A History of American Philosophy, c. 34 (1946).

their individual freedoms. The citizen realizes himself in the achievements of the state, or if he does not in fact he will be conclusively presumed to do so in contemplation of law. Thus the loss of his liberties can be the means conceived to establish liberty.

It is significant that all these schools have addressed themselves not so much to freedom itself as to what they consider to be its conditions precedent. Perhaps they have been wise to avoid defining their ultimate goals, for freedom, of all concepts, is probably the hardest to put into a verbal formula. Nevertheless, if we could even outline what we mean by the word, our analysis would become much more profitable. The end we desire may or may not justify the means we select to achieve it; but, if we understand the end, we know at least what methods are at hand to choose from. So we ought to begin by asking: Within the areas of human experience to which law attaches, what is meant by the desire to be free?

The genesis of the impulse contains a significant clue. Our first active manifestation of life is the urge to get out of the confining womb. As Donne says, " we are all conceived in close prison " and with a hatred of walls. In a very young infant a loud noise or sudden loss of support will bring fear reactions; they convey threats to physical security, to safe order. But hold the infant too tightly, so as to hamper its bodily movements, and the reactions will be those of rage: " the stiffening of the whole body, the free slashing movements of hands, arms and legs, and the holding of the breath. . . . until the face appears blue." [2] The kick against the walls goes through life.

[2] Watson, Behaviorism 8–9, 122–24 (1924).

As the human being matures, his urge to be free pervades every level of his being. A claustrophobia is felt in his mind, which writhes and squirms to break confinement, even the confinement of its own perspective as fixed by time and place. His emotional organism, with its great impulsive forces, fights against society's rigid stockades, and casts its acid of satire and ridicule over their bounds. Men are rebellious in all their parts. They need the ability to move, which we call freedom.

Now, of course, time, space, and circumstance are coordinates of any working freedom. One man's mobility in his setting is another's servitude in his. Order, likewise, is relative to the felt needs of the here-and-now, the demands of land, streets, and machines. But all legal settings are similar in so far as they must include men. Though strong human urges may be diverted by a property tenure system or a state order, they will press against such channels, erode the walls, and even overflow them. The will to be free does not die out, though it may temporarily subside. It is an operative element in every juridical complex.

Mobility acquires its relevance when an issue arises in a specific surrounding. To be free would be only a conceptual state unless the occasion to move somehow offered itself. But since mobility has an origin in the muscles, it is susceptible of atrophy, and freedom long unused may dry up and wither. Freedom in law is therefore readiness for the issue, capacity to move not too infrequently exercised. That is doubtless why the legend tells us that Prometheus on the mountainside keeps straining at his unbreakable bonds. Whether he would do good or harm if he were liberated is not material to the notion of freedom.

Meanwhile, the social order which confines the areas of mobility also makes mobility possible. In a mature society at least, the movement of things, men, and ideas is facilitated to an astonishing degree by the techniques of organized control. Only when a given society breaks down is the full extent of this dependence disclosed, and even then in part only for no breakdown of more than momentary duration can be nearly complete. But the occasions of social dissolution might serve to illustrate how order and freedom are related to each other. Perhaps in the operation of law, freedom and order are not irreconcilable, and beyond Athens with its chaotic liberty, its Alcibiades, and its Peloponnesian disaster, beyond Sparta with its gray discipline, its cultural stagnation, and its Leuctra, there is a third possibility.

II. *Mobility in Law and Society*

Freedom has high survival potence. Trees die when their roots can no longer expand to draw nourishment; insects, birds, and animals must move where safety and food are to be found. The infinitely elaborate processes of agriculture, manufacture, and distribution are all designs in motion and so are the operations of education, the arts, and government itself. A legal code enforced to cut off movement might strangle the life of men. But freedom may also work destruction on those who exercise it. The insect that moves loses the advantages of protective coloration; the roving beast forfeits the safety of his lair; men when they wander risk being injured or killed; and a society, if it breaks basic patterns and releases lawless impulsions, can dissolve into chaos. Mobility is essential to human organization, the creative and progressive genius of man is bound up in it; but, like all concepts of power, it comprises evil as well as good. Freedom by itself is only potentiality; mere mobility in the law is to be desired only because it is indispensable.

Movement of Things. The law imposes its rules upon the movement of things. In fact, one of the most ancient and universal legal notions is that of theft; *i.e.*, the taking away of a thing against its possessor's will. Theft is forbidden in the interest of human beings, not of objects; the law is not concerned with the absolute location of things, but with their location vis-à-vis relevant persons. It is interested in those whom movement may affect, those who would use or consume the thing, or might suffer from its proximity. In our present system, the legal interest extends to persons who, regardless of possible consumption or pragmatic use, have acquired a relation of recognized mastery toward the thing. The wills and imaginations of men invest the location of things with a juridic meaning. Hence the Civil Law rightly distinguishes between " immovable and movable," not real and personal property.

What is a thing? A child may think it knows, but the law is unsure. It may treat a ship [3] or a sword as a person, it may attach unique magic to the segments of a slain animal, [4] or it may decide that striking a harnessed horse is an assault on human occupants of the carriage. [5] On the other

[3] The jural personification of inanimate things is discussed by John Chipman Gray, The Nature and Sources of the Law 46, *et seq.* (2d ed. 1921).

[4] The Biblical Covenant of the Pieces, Genesis 15.9; Jeremiah 34.18; Plato, Laws 753D; Livy XL. 5, 6.

[5] Bull v. Colton, 22 Barb. 94 (N. Y. Sup. Ct. 1856).

hand, as far back as we can peer into the dimness of antiquity and ever since, the law has disposed of certain human beings as though they were things. Not only in legendary Rome, but likewise in early Russia, China, India, and Brazil abduction of the bride was the customary technique of marriage. Forcibly carried to her new home, she was lifted over the threshold (as today) to symbolize change of ownership.

Slaves too were things in the law, and our state courts experienced some perplexity in classifying them as real or personal. Livy tells us of the solemn grant of a whole nation,[6] an event that has its analogues in recent history. And perhaps it is tactless to recall that in 1941 the United States Supreme Court, holding that California could not close its borders to needy Americans, based the decision on the commerce clause of the Constitution.[7]

Progressively as man has acquired more sophisticated mastery over things, he has objected to being treated as one in law. So long as he could carve an image out of wood and then whine and cringe before his own artifice, a thing could be regarded as self-important, as an end. Legal anal-

[6] VII. 30, 31. A conquered people surrendered by going through the formal ceremony of *stipulatio,* identical with that by which a private party might undertake unilaterally to pay a specified sum of money. Nussbaum, A Concise History of the Law of Nations 17 (1947). The individual citizens of the conquered nation (*dediticii*) remained, until rather late in the Empire, close to serfdom and did not enjoy even peregrine status. Buckland, A Text-Book of Roman Law from Augustus to Justinian 96–99 (2d ed. 1932).

[7] A California law made it a crime to bring any indigent nonresident into the state. The majority of the Supreme Court held this law to be a burden on interstate commerce which the state could not constitutionally impose. Edwards v. California, 314 U. S. 160 (1941). Justices Douglas, Black, Murphy, and Jackson, agreeing with the result, insisted that the constitutional right of free migration should be based rather on the individual's citizenship in the nation.

ogy to it was not utterly degrading. But recent centuries have brought the realization that technical craftsmanship is a species of almost complete mastery. The material object is now so plastic to man's will that it loses its own magic and shapes itself to his. It becomes pure instrument. On the other hand, while human beings often serve to implement the purposes of others, they can never wholly cease to project their own. Unless they have a turn to play designer and master, they twist in the hand and spoil the work.

The legal regulation of the movement of things concerns itself with man as consumer, craftsman, and barterer. It follows the directions of his interests and capabilities as such. Some things move faster under his growing skill, and then the law must reduce its emphasis on possession, continuity of outward appearance, and other attributes of a slower rhythm. Such problems are eventually graduated to the realm of titles, which can be observed and controlled at a rapid pace.

Superficially things of the same kind and quality are fungible in the courts; one is the equivalent of any other. But just because the intention of law is human manipulation or consumption, time and space become co-ordinates in the jural Gestalt. Slaves have been known to escape to free soil; strawberries are perishable; time changes the market price of uranium. Moreover, accessibility of goods may depend upon their location — not absolutely, but with regard to the parties, their markets and profits. A contract for the future delivery of cotton will not feed the looms. Thus courts cannot a priori equate many species of things without view to date and location. Movement, which is the change of location in time, is a factor in the operative rule of law.

This is the same movement that law itself can stimulate or retard. Since Joseph in Egypt, government has set the metronome for the distribution of materials. Things may be legally barred from the country or their import subjected to heavy duty; things may be shipped away in conformity with official inducements; things may never come into being because the law prohibits them or subsidizes their competitors. As society becomes more highly industrialized, the movement grows faster and more sensitive. Merchandise increases impressively in mass and variety, but sterner regulation forces it into fewer and closer channels of manufacture and marketing. This is mobility indeed, but in predetermined directions. Freedom bears in its own dynamism the necessity of control.

This same mobility reacts upon and reshapes the law. Large segments of tort and criminal law are by-products of the automobile. The doctrine of contracts had already met the stagecoach and was ready for railroads. The aeroplane has recently ripped heaven off the fee simple, and perhaps nuclear fission will take care of the balance. In any event, when movement attains a certain high rate of speed, national society replaces the citizen as craftsman and offers a much wider scope for mobility without damage. But the more violent physical forces do not seem to keep accurately informed of boundaries, even the most sovereign.

In our system, contract law embraces most aspects of man's mastery of things. This mastery is the progressively elaborate product of combined human wills. The technique of combination is a congeries of contracts covering every tedious step from the original blueprint to the completed machine for making blueprints. But, as time goes on, the familiar forms of contract grow old, obsolete, and forgotten; others emerge and evolve, meeting the occasions of a new time that never remains. The meaning of contract itself has modified along with the instances; the available choice becomes narrower and the legal implications of making a choice become more ramified. When the traditional nomenclature is preserved, it is at the cost of a changed functional reference. Ultimately, the movement of things may be found completely controlled by the rules of administrative agencies. If that should come to be, the historic process will have culminated — slow, largely undirected mobility of things will have been transferred for directed speed. In terms of human freedom, the exchange need not entail net loss.

Movement of Intangibles. Mobility is not confined to what the hand can grasp, because the human being who is a craftsman and consumer is also a symbolist. Material things are given him through the world of sense, but he creates his own symbols, manipulates them, and even submits his life to their rule. He surrounds himself with a realm of meaningful signs, and builds civilization out of their thin substance. Symbols are the girders of society, fitted together to maintain a rational order, shifted or torn apart when new symbols promise a higher eminence.

Concerning the movement of intangibles, the early law was characteristically clumsy.[8] In the first place, the title

[8] Holmes's is, of course, the classic statement of this dilemma and of the analogies employed in resolving it. The Common Law, lectures VI, X, and XI (1881).

to an object of religious awe could not be transferred, for how could human rules control what had been invested with the magic of the god? This superstitious impediment has endured: even today ecclesiastical title or mortmain immobilizes the use of valuable structures and men blow on their hands while some strange god sits in warmth. Moreover, although nonreligious material things could, understandably to the primitive mind, take a new owner along with a new custody, there seemed no way to transfer the law's own creatures; *i.e.*, the many intangible rights that accrue in an evolving economic system. How could one hand over what he could not handle?

At long last the necessary techniques were acquired; the transfer of intangible rights was found to have its analogies in the usual forms of sales or in succession by inheritance of property. But since in all conscience lawyers remember better than they learn, the process was painfully slow. Nor is it yet quite complete, for certain intangibles are still inalienable. On the whole, however, owners have learned to transfer titles and legal claims as freely as the things for which they stand. Ingenuity has endowed the written assignment and the instrument payable to bearer with a subtle magic.

Clever magicians never believe implicitly in their own prestidigitation. The law had always restricted free alienation of property — in the interest of feudal rights, or of family solidarity, or of the claims of creditors. Mobility of titles was habitually hedged about by principles of judicial policy; the performance had its fixed rules. But in recent times the contest has grown much sharper between the inventive hand of the legal profession and the eye of state regulation. In antimonopoly administration, in control of currency and securities, and in tax law, the mobility of titles has been decisively impaired.[9] It is one of the revealing paradoxes of our system that, while so many citizens strive to acquire property titles, others find no way to get rid of theirs.

A specious mobility may work harm. Certain conventional symbols of ownership have been drawn farther and farther from their true objects of reference, which begin to fade out of notice. Owners of expensive voting trust certificates and suchlike corporate paper find themselves remote indeed from anything to possess, manage, or use. Mobility of titles then proves to be an optical illusion: beneath the fluid surface whatever is substantial remains motionless. There is jeopardy here for the institutional basis of property. Trends that divorce exchange value from economic utility confront the legal system with a radical choice. Where law is compelled to focus on one and miss the other, it must ultimately turn toward economic worth. The process of title attenuation has not yet affected all aspects of ownership; but all are as vulnerable as Antaeus when they are lifted too long from the ground.

Over against this acceleration of movement in private titles, there flows a contrary current. In every mature economy, public ownership envelops more and more land, more residential, cultural, and industrial installations. Such titles are almost irrevocably immobilized; they subsist but do not pass. Exchange, speculation, commerce, and commercial law can no longer reckon with them, except however in

[9] That is, a transfer effectual for all other jural purposes is ignored in enforcing the pertinent regulation or tax.

terms of their new significance. Their mobility relates now to goods and services, and to the varying projects of government. Maximum immobility of title may be made consistent here with the free flow of human satisfactions.

Thus, despite the frenetic speed of transactions in stocks and contracts for commodities, the aggregate mobility of titles would appear to have passed its zenith in our legal order. In time, many intangibles may become as immobile as they were in primitive law, but not by reason of religious awe or technical ineptitude. Whether the process will justify itself in pragmatic advance depends upon the wisdom of those concerned, for the evidence does not show that man's freedom is welded to any particular system of property tenure.

Titles are by no means the only juridic symbols that society has evolved. In fact, the human will manifests itself more clearly in formal emblems of assent; it may attain creative force when it acts to become bound mutually with others. Agreements, great or small, are the very fibers and sinews of the legal order. They transmit its effectuality and enable men to convert their separate lacks into a common profit. But every promise has its cost: it usurps the roles of time and destiny. By promising, a man surrenders something that is undisclosed and potential for something that is determinate and reciprocal. Thus he commits a segment of his future. If later the promise is not performed, what can be done to enforce that commitment?

Now, of course, the historic legal systems have not been equally sensitive to the sanctity of contracts. Early law had to place heavy reliance on solemn oaths and conditional curses (calculated to involve fates and furies in any subsequent litigation),[10] and on the more practical assurance of holding a pledge or a hostage. Another technique, coolly realistic, consisted in enslaving the defaulting debtor to his creditor; but this program for the payment of debts was not applied to obligors of superior caste — they paid only as they wished. In India it was customary to sit on the debtor's doorstep and threaten to fast to death there unless paid,[11] a somewhat dramatic style of dunning which has not proved popular in other lands. In general, the notion that the debtor's own body stands responsible for his debts has enjoyed particular appeal: an Englishman's land well into the nineteenth century was considerably safer than his skin from the exactions of creditors. For that matter, even if he broke a contract to sell his land, an equity court would, under the ironic heading of "specific performance," put him in jail but leave the land alone.

Nineteenth-century reforms did much to relieve the body of the debtor in exchange for more extensive access to his real and personal property. As time went on, money was treated as adequate to satisfy all kinds of claims; and when the Federal Congress during the American Civil War authorized acceptance of $300 as a substitute for military service, the capacity of a man's property to answer for his obligations attained vertiginous heights. Finally, a distin-

---

[10] Hence the heavy emphasis in all early codes and treaties on the sacrilegious horror of broken or perjurious oaths. Art. 108 of the Laws of Manu provided: " The witness to whom, within seven days after he has given evidence, happens (a misfortune through) sickness, a fire, or the death of a relative, shall be made to pay the debt and a fine." The medieval trials by ordeal likewise assumed that Providence was immediately concerned with the validity of each individual swearing. Like ourselves, Plato thought Providence was more importantly occupied, and accordingly proposed to abolish litigants' oaths. Laws 948D.

[11] Rankin, Background to Indian Law 212-13 (1946).

guished veteran of that war ventured to equate all legally binding promises with the promisor's " assumption of risk " to pay damages " if the promised event should not come to pass." [12]   The most aspiring covenant then became a mere conditional obligation to deliver money.

Holmes's doctrine, after a brief day of credulous popularity, has been confined by critical studies to its legitimate bounds.   Here we are not concerned with the technical shortcomings of a theory, but with what has happened to breach of contract in the ensuing years.   In private transactions the mass production of potentially dangerous commodities and machines has evoked a new series of implied warranties, imposed by the law of the situation upon manufacturers and vendors.   These warranties and the heavy obligations they entail may be regarded as instances of Holmes's " assumed risk "; but when, as now so often happens in times of emergency, the manufacturer's license is forfeited, his produce is embargoed, or his plant is taken over by the government because he has lightly chosen to assume too many risks, it will avail him little to acknowledge a conditional liability to pay money damages.   And as the network of general economic interdependence becomes more evident, those who can produce what society considers its bread and butter, and even some varieties of its jam, likewise will not be heard to proffer their own losses as damages that will compensate the public's deprivation. The push is toward genuine " specific performance " of tasks assigned by the social order and, where consent continues to be relevant at all, it may pertain only to the acceptance of the assignment.

[12] Holmes, The Common Law, lecture VIII (1881).

Thus the role of contractual promise tends to shrink in our economy; the traditional legal phrase " bargain and sale " is heard rather seldom in a vocabulary of mass production and chain distribution. Bargains there may be, sales there must be; but of free negotiation and bargaining between the buyer and the seller there is notably less. In the process, an assumed " right " to respond in money damages (like the " right " to abstain from work and from the food that work purchases) cannot last long. To some these movements will disagreeably resemble confiscation or involuntary servitude; to all they imply a transformation of received values. If as always in man's history there is to be undesired service, it may be directed to enhance the *general* welfare only.[13] On those terms, the new values can include a working degree of mobility.

Movement of Persons — Horizontal. We approach that portion of our topic which, because it deals with human beings as subjects of mobility, should begin to bring the whole study into focus. Up to this point, movement has been studied in terms of its eventual impact on persons, and its significance has been analyzed out of the consequences of that impact. In this section man not only composes the drama, directs its production, and gains or loses by its reception; he personally enacts it. His role calls for two different yet obviously related species of movement: the movement of a man from place to place over the surface of the earth (horizontal), and his movement up and down in relation to the structure of his society (vertical).[14] The

[13] Involuntary service for *public* purposes has always been part of pioneer democracy. See the Massachusetts Body of Liberties, Art. 5 (1641).

[14] This nomenclature follows that established by Sorokin, Social Mobility (1927), except that horizontal mobility is not confined here to move-

two movements, each functionally tied to the other, sum up a human being's course in life.

At the outset one is struck by the connection between horizontal mobility and social esteem. Mobility is considered to be an ensign of nobility. The man who can move about more quickly by means of a horse, an automobile, a tank, or a plane enjoys some of the legendary magic of seven-league boots, of messenger demigods, and winged angels. The *eques*, the knight, and the cavalryman traditionally are in a position to look down on the sluggish infantry. They can go wherever they want — and so much faster. By the same token, in law the dignity of a sovereign is affected by the right of his ambassadors to move about freely.

But mobility has a polar aspect that suggests its inner meaning. Not all movement wins regard. In fact, the vagabond — tramp, gypsy, or nomad — may be the refuse of society. Men sit in their homes and shake their heads as they see the waifs come and go. For despite our universal itch of restlessness, mere aimless moving (like the " *circulez!* " of the policeman) implies a hopeless and pathetic state. Thus horizontal mobility derives its prestige from the fact that some particular destination is contemplated. " To depart " may or may not be estimable; " to set forth " always is, whatever the chosen objective.

In the brief span of legal history, horizontal mobility appears scarce indeed for major segments of mankind. Hannibal, by devastating the Italian peninsula, unintentionally transformed Roman agriculture into a system of large-scale

---

ment within the bounds of a single society. Sociologists appear to have strangely neglected the influence of law on social mobility.

industrialized production.   This shortly necessitated importing servile labor.   From then on, through the eras of vast *latifundia* and down to the disruptive shock of the Black Death, a large part of each passing generation was fixed to the soil, wearing out the years of its age within the scenes of some isolated parish.   How that servitude fastened both provincialism and authoritarianism on Western society is, of course, a familiar narrative; [15] but no historian could do justice to the myriad personal frustrations woven in.   Horizontal immobility was almost certain to produce bitter psychic effects.   It long exaggerated the force and stretched the duration of paternal and ecclesiastical authority.   It shrank the horizons for individual self-validation. No wonder that Western man, once enabled to pierce the boundaries of his little county, did not stop until he had crossed the seas, discovered the Indies, settled the Antipodes, and challenged the poles.

Modern constitutional law is particularly indebted to horizontal mobility.   As Plato recognized when he described his " second best state," the setting out on an expedition of conquest, migration, or colonization is a critical occasion for making constitutions.   Men can then exchange the institutions they have inherited for new ones of their own choice.   The slate, though not wholly clear, will show bare spaces where the desired precepts may be filled in.   Thus horizontal movement offers the opportunity for consent rather than custom to shape a rising social system. And where the migration, like that to America, has been across broad water, it has broken up families, tribes, and

---

[15] Kardiner, The Psychological Frontiers of Society 409 (1945). *See* lex Salica, tit. XLV.

other cohesive groups; it has invited the venturers to agree upon and jointly create a new order. War, too, and economic turmoil have frequently generated constitutions, but in such circumstances the framers are likely to be fettered with the beliefs and practices of the existing regime. Migration, on the other hand, invokes boldness. Its analogue is the complete ruin of the previous structure (France in 1789), or the lapse of sufficient time before drafting the new constitution so that it can be adapted to a transformed order (the United States in 1787 or the Soviet Union in 1936). Such are the conditions that make constitutional ground shake under foot.

While history talks in gross, men live in detail. Horizontal mobility would concern them much less if it were merely an attribute of the mass. The individual, however, hardly remains frozen awaiting a *Völkerwanderung*. As the empty spaces of the globe are progressively occupied, mass migration will probably diminish in importance. One may even hope that the coerced resettlement of whole populations will no longer disgrace our civilization. If so, the nuclear value of free movement will be sought in the life of the individual, and he in turn will convert that value into certain critical questions: (1) Can he migrate to any land of his choice? (2) Can he move about and live where he pleases in the country of his birth or adoption? (3) Can he emigrate at will?

Pursuing these inquiries, the future legal historian may read his notes with a sardonic smile. He will be intrigued by the contrast in our times between brave paper pronouncements on the one hand and the daily operation of national laws on the other. His notes will show a sharp parabolic rise in the causes that prompt individuals to migrate. Lands of milk and honey have beckoned, while modern transportation has evolved into a swift magic carpet. With the solidifying of national boundaries, mass movement has been blocked and men can migrate only as individuals. But the notes will also show that immigration has been minimized or barred even by sparsely settled countries (Canada, Australia, Argentina); that mobility within native or adopted territory has been made a matter of race (Union of South Africa); that the right of expatriation is dubious a century and a quarter after it was fought over in the War of 1812; and that emigration, when physically possible, may jeopardize the individual's civil status and property (the Soviet Union). In regard to the United States, the relevant items will include: the segregation, during the Second World War, of citizens of Japanese descent; California's attempt to impose property qualifications on impoverished citizens desiring to enter the state; [16] and the segregation of Negro citizens in residential areas, schools, conveyances, inns, and theaters. Of course, any outline of the discriminations against noncitizens will offer an interesting commentary on the notion that all men are created equal. The historian may conclude that legal immobility is the characteristic paradox of our technologically mobile epoch.

But an objective judgment will weigh some additional considerations. It will regard the harsher impediments to free movement not as immutable but as concomitants of a social lag. The lag in the law may not shrink during the years ahead, but there are indications that it can. For in-

[16] *See* note 7 *supra.*

stance, in the United States discriminatory covenants in deeds of property may no longer be enforced by the courts. There are reasons to believe that, where the impediments to free movement are mere accidental constructs of a federal system, they have to yield gradually to the centripetal forces within our economy.

Moreover, the majority of men (it is not *malum in se* to be a member of the majority) do enjoy more horizontal mobility than in ages past. And in a given country, the legally effective majority is itself a sum of minorities, compounded quite recently as various disqualifications of sex, race, property, religion, and national origin have been set aside. At this stage, race and political belief are the most invidious remaining prejudices, and since they are not new but very old the blurring of the other ancient differentiae may justify an expectation of the same fate for them. The eventual cure for minority pangs can be found in an expanding majority, one that takes more and more species into its genus. But this still seems to call for a wry sort of patience, notwithstanding some twenty-three centuries of brief exertion and long sloth.

Immigration, free domestic movement, and the right to emigrate have obvious psychic and constitutional values. They confer an aura of consent upon the state. They clothe force and utility in moral robes and ease the conscience of a majority that is determined to have its own way. If one can emigrate at will, he does enjoy a choice of alternatives. If then he remains, consent is likely to be attributed to him, and the governors of the state are deemed entitled to full obedience. Socrates, as he awaited execution, made this very argument in defense of the Athenian laws;[17] Cicero, Vattel, and Jefferson regarded emigration as a natural right. Certain it is that " a state which denies to its citizens the right to emigrate reduces itself to the level of a prison." [18] Loyalty to such a state is, like the loyalty of a prison trusty, somewhat brittle; the wardens must live nervously and walk with suspicion.

In the experience, however, of most normal individuals, horizontal mobility does not have such lofty connotations. Outside the scope of curiosity and restlessness, its main significance is in relation to vertical mobility. Most men wish to remove in order to move upward in life, to " better themselves " (*i.e.*, their pocketbooks). In this aspect our panorama acquires a third dimension.

Movement of Persons — Vertical. It is customary, in expositions of relativity in physics, to present the problem of an object moving within a laboratory or chamber that is itself in movement. The vector value of a moving object in such a laboratory should be stated in terms of both movements; it cannot be adequately explained by either alone. Now, obviously, the same approach is indispensable to any description of the vertical movement of men. They move up and down (1) as the total society rises and falls in respect to prosperity, technique, and culture, (2) as their particular social and economic groups rise and fall in relation to the balance of society, and (3) as they in their individual careers rise and fall within a group, penetrate into other groups, or pursue a course of apparent but unreal isolation. The legal fabric impinges heavily on each of these movements.

[17] Crito 50, *et seq.*
[18] Lauterpacht, An International Bill of the Rights of Man 130 (1945).

Public economic and fiscal legislation has, of course, much to do with the general movement of organic society and, by like token, with the position of its members. An unintelligent tariff measure may impoverish the economy, and a shrewd exploitation of water power may enrich it. But given some specific level of social welfare, the critical question for law is the incidence of the goods and services that are available at any particular time. Are they to be distributed and, if so, on what terms? Is distribution, as in the case of schooling and vaccination, to be made compulsory? Are patent monopolies to be granted? How may they be used and to what ends? It is apparent that in an industrialized, compact society the vertical movement of individuals may be directly altered by the law governing discoveries and new accessions.

The law also controls the relative movement of economic groups, the nuclei of assembled power. When the collective privileges of labor unions are increased by the law, each member moves vertically in relation to unorganized workers and the balance of the citizenry. When financial or industrial trusts are dissolved, the members move down, in terms of power at least. But whatever the influence of groups, the career which interests the individual (specifically the American) is that which he can carve for himself within the larger framework. The general advance of society and the progress of his association are genuinely meaningful, but his gaze is centered on his own prospects. The chance to create and to climb is the very essence of his view of freedom; and in that view his legal system must exhibit its ultimate worth through the vertical mobility it makes possible.

The attitude men evince toward vertical mobility shows the *mores*, the *morale*, and the *morality* of their society. The *mores* determine which human qualities shall make for movement up or down in the communal structure. In times of widespread corruption or revolution, when the lees of society are churned up, the rewards will go to strong, aggressive personalities who may commit every offense so long as they are not guilty of hesitation. Then vertical mobility is rapid indeed; titles, offices, and estates arise and crumble overnight. In such times the law is weak or silent; it can only mumble like an old man whose glands have failed. Such periods of dissolution teach us that ineffectual law may be brushed aside as a regulator of vertical movement, but not how law operates in the eras when it really controls human conduct. The mores of these eras are more instructive.

Virtually all traditional fields of law in a society apply its mores to vertical mobility. Rules of law tell the citizen how he may rise or fall. The prohibitions of the criminal code affect his course directly but negatively; the tenets and institutions of civil law show him the positive path. A man may make his way in the world by means of the institution of dowry or by entering into lawful miscegenation.[19] He may rise by inheritance or gift, election or appointment, slander or fraud, performance or breach of trust, conversion of bailment, fidelity or betrayal in all the ramified relations that invoke the approval or punishment of the law. Most rapidly of all, he may step up or down by contract. Executory contract is the chief elevator in

[19] For the contribution of miscegenation to social mobility in Brazil, *see* Freyre, The Masters and the Slaves, cc. I–II (1946).

Western society, though, of course, those who enter it can only guess whether a particular agreement will take them up or down. That being the case, it is shrewd foresight and audacity that our legal system favors, even more than predatory skill in persuading customers and eliminating competitors. And these favored qualities seem likely to retain their advantage under other property systems, though their emolument might consist in special housing, privileged purchasing status, vacation advantages, managerial authority, and other nonpecuniary premiums.

The *morale* of a society is tested by its emphasis on upward movement. A red-blooded economy, full of self-confidence, will regard the opportunity for individual advancement well worth the cost of some incidental tragedies. It is accustomed to see its future leaders clambering up a ladder of corpses. Mobility for them is then the keynote of the legal system. During this phase of Anglo-Saxon history, *caveat emptor* became an article of faith; adequacy of consideration in contracts was deemed no concern of the courts; and restrictions on testamentary disposition were removed. The ancient stratifications were to be torn away and every man was to be given some chance in the contest. But a condition was attached: He must not whimper if he lost, no matter how adventitious or disproportionate his disaster. He must not look to the courts if he were ripped, for law and equity (which was said to " follow the law ") would stoically shield their eyes. And this robust neutrality continued until it came to be perverted by its own beneficiaries. The winners in the race for business success, finally wearying, asked the judges to perpetuate their leads by enjoining interference with established advantageous relations, and the courts, always respectful of possession, made it a policy to comply. This is an evidence of incipient social anemia.

Where the society has a thin-blooded morale, it will attempt to block individual ascent. Law then closes the professions and the civil service to many classes; it freezes salaries and enforces the relational order that it finds. Property passes entailed, testamentary disposition is largely predetermined, guild obligations are strict and formalized. Individuals can move only with the group to which the law has assigned them. These precautions succeed in holding down creative skill and talent; there remains only one way to rise quickly, and that is by knowing the people who will be useful in circumventing the law.

The *morality* of society is reflected in its attitude toward failure, the vertical descent. Many must lose the struggle for the prize, and some will lose before they have fairly begun. If the community has a conscience, it will provide sympathetically for these. If it is intelligent, it will acknowledge how many it has crippled at the start or has tripped. If it is self-critical, it will investigate whether the main contest for success is a desirable one. Bankruptcy laws and social-security provisions, for example, are ways of mitigating the loss, not of palliating the wrong.

We can readily see that the law profoundly affects the chances of ascent and the consequences of fall. What is most important is that it regulates the tempo of vertical movement. Society cannot stand the disruption of an excessive speed in personal advancement or the corrosive envy that too much speed incites. To watch a meteor is to fear collision and to hope for its distant fall. As Leonardo said: " He who wishes to become rich in a day is hanged in a year." He is hanged because restraints must be imposed on acquisitive skill, on demagogic personality, on commercial as well as political Catilinism. Society needs a chance to absorb the commotion; neighbors need a chance to digest the evidence of the fortunate one's superiority.[20]

Taxation has become the prime technique for regulation of the speed of ascent. Through it the rate of movement of social classes can be controlled to a considerable degree; the distribution of general goods and gains can be partially predetermined. In the case of individuals, the impact is most cogent where the tax is progressive. Charging a man on each dollar according to the amount of his other dollars of income, inheritance, or capital slows the impetus of his advance. He is handicapped by the weight of his own acquisitions, and the farther he moves the less each additional step will carry him. If the incremental dollars look like a windfall, then he may be relieved of them all. Wartime and postwar excess-profits taxes were designed to effectuate this kind of policy: by exempting the average income earned during some previous " normal " period and by taking most of the excess, they retarded the accumulation of wealth. For if not all bigness is a curse, sudden bigness is quite likely to be.

Now it becomes apparent that Maine's famous apothegm (" from status to contract ") was a bold formula to de-

[20] Respecting our own profession, Tacitus tells us of two eminent lawyers, Labeo Antistius and Capito Ateius, one of whom gained popularity by being deferred in advancement, the other envy and hatred by being advanced too fast. Annals III. lxxv. Modern instances can be readily supplied out of the reader's experience.

scribe the nineteenth-century increase in vertical mobility. That formula has been contradicted by successive developments of the past two generations, as elements of status have been written into one contract after another; and, whatever its partial truth, it failed to allow for the general movement of the social chamber within which any individual ascent must take place. As these developments show, there is no profit in trying to find a simple formula for the infinitely complex data of legal history. Clio is a notoriously accommodating witness; she is willing to vouch for any man's thesis. But without generalizing too widely, we may infer that vertical mobility is indispensable to the health of a society, and that a tenure system which does not allow it creates grave risks.

Movement of Ideas. Legal regulation of movement has nowhere been so self-conscious as in the realm of ideas. The monumental literature of the subject is familiar enough so that we can dispense with repetition and concentrate on certain facets which have been partially neglected. It will always be important to recall that the movement of ideas, which we usually call " free expression," kindles from the rebelliousness in the human make-up, the resentment of prohibitions. Adam must have been intended to taste the fruit of the tree of knowledge or he would not have been forbidden it. Free expression touches the irreverent, anarchic, and disbelieving first, the denial before the affirmation.

Now, historically speaking, the notion that all men should be free to communicate irreverent ideas has never been popular with either ecclesiastical or secular law. And although since the era of *Areopagitica* there have appeared many exalted manifestos, both literary and constitutional, proclaiming a sacred right of iconoclasm, these seem in practical application to be addressed to the idols of the past, not to those of the current milieu. Everyone is free now to discuss transubstantiation or the divine right of kings, conceptualism or the merits of the manorial system, though topics like these are covered with some ancient bloodstains. The problem of mobility does not arise unless the intellectual issue under consideration pinches here and now. For example, the presently applicable criterion in the Southern states is what may be said not concerning Negro slavery but concerning Negro segregation. Each society shows its temper in respect to certain of its own institutions, those specifically which it considers to be most vulnerable.

These prized institutions have almost always been ruled by a specified elite [21] (secular or clerical, elected or imposed). That elite regards governing as its characteristic function, and the right to criticize or evaluate as its monopoly. If it performs its function competently, it can hardly be expected to welcome criticism from outside its ranks; if it is incompetent, fear and guilt will prompt it to suppress criticism. In any event, since gradations of political wisdom are recognized everywhere, the outsider's opinion will be subject to discount even within a democracy. Hence, criticism from a nonelite source is never considered sufficiently valuable to outweigh all other interests; it is usually impeded by private interests (*e.g.*, it must not violate the law of defamation) and universally by public in-

[21] This term is used neither in commendation nor ironic disparagement, but simply to connote the division of social functions. A valuable sidelight is cast by Franz Kafka's The Problem of Our Laws in The Great Wall of China 254 (1946).

terests (*e.g.*, it must not involve an incitement to riot).

Moreover, mobility of ideas has been profoundly affected by the rise of the nation-state. Our legal systems are, for all effectual purposes, in the hands of national governments, which have a way of regarding subversion or treason as the highest crime a subject can commit. But the subject is a human being and by that title has attributes and values which transcend the national. National law can thus become quite incongruous to him, for, as Professor Whitehead says, " beyond Caesar there stretches the array of aspirations whose coordinating principle is termed God." [22] And in this respect even an international government could only reduce the measure of inadequacy, for no matter how broad or numerous the categories we devise for men there will remain some residue that refuses subsumption.

Mobility in simple communication may be differentiated into the following rights:

1. To stand silent
2. To express oneself by speaking or writing
3. To persuade or inform
4. Not to hear
5. To express oneself by hearing or reading
6. To be persuaded or informed
7. To receive an ideological variety

Libertarians in the centuries that witnessed the emergence of nation-states were preoccupied with the first three of these rights, with perhaps some desultory patronage for the fifth. But only the rise of our technological cacophony could make the fourth so precious that, a generation ago,

[22] Whitehead, Essays in Science and Philosophy 65 (1947).

Justice Brandeis spoke of it (" the right to be let alone ") as " the most comprehensive of rights and the right most valued by civilized man." [23]   His appraisal has not been vindicated, for the right not to hear has yielded in law to the right of others, particularly where garbed in religious or antireligious vestments, to persuade or inform.   Uncomfortable as this may leave " civilized man," the legal trend conforms to a universal coalescence.

The grand issues of the future relate, of course, to the sixth and seventh rights; *i.e.*, the right to be persuaded or informed, and the right to receive an ideological variety. The former has gained its initial recognition in the Supreme Court's *Tucker* and *Marsh* opinions.[24]   The Court there sustained the constitutional freedom of Jehovah's Witnesses to propagandize on government property and in a privately owned company town, reasoning in its opinion that the *residents* of these areas had a right to the opportunity to be persuaded or informed.   Since the residents were not before the Court as parties to the litigation, the rationale apparently presumes (rather conclusively, in view of the unpopularity of the Witnesses' methods) that the *prospective recipient* of opinion or information desires to receive it, and that his interest in being exposed to new ideas or facts has a constitutional foundation.   And this presumption will likely expand to the very limits of its

---

[23] Olmstead v. United States, 277 U. S. 438, 478–79 (1928).

[24] In the *Tucker* case the defendant, contrary to the order of the manager of a village built on government land to house defense workers, called at the doors of the residents, stated his views, and distributed his printed matter.   In the *Marsh* case the facts were similar, except that the activities took place on the sidewalk of a town owned by a shipbuilding corporation. The Supreme Court held that these activities could not constitutionally be punished.   Tucker v. Texas, 326 U. S. 517 (1946); Marsh v. Alabama, 326 U. S. 501 (1946).

basin; it has already begun to spill over to international transmission of news.[25]

The right to receive an ideological variety has fared poorly everywhere. The initiation of compulsory education and the resultant general rise of literacy have caused ruling elites to emphasize indoctrination in approved dogmas. In the United States concentration of ownership of newspaper and radio chains has established conditions suitable to herd thinking. The Supreme Court has been alert to defend freedom of expression by the press, and to resist monopoly in the distribution of public information; but in society's most sensitive area — the field of child education — it has failed to devise a shield against ideological monopoly.[26]

Now, it is well to note that we are dealing here with a mobility which wins more praise in print than active devotion in daily life. To criticize the government may be healthful — everyone everywhere enjoys grumbling. Most individuals are, however, too busy with the advancement of their own careers, too deeply enmeshed in the trammels of industrialized living, to enlist in the greater political conflicts. In that sense perhaps " there was more diffused freedom in the City of London in the year 1633, when Charles the First was King, than there is today in any industrial city of the world." [27]   It is the elite that have the time as well as the aptitude, the control of the radio stentor as well as the will to rule and the pragmatic plans.

[25] *See* Article 19 of the Universal Declaration of Human Rights, adopted by the General Assembly of the United Nations on December 10, 1948. 6 U. N. Bull. 7 (1949).

[26] Pierce v. Society of Sisters, 268 U. S. 510 (1925), discussed at p. 6, note 3 *supra*.

[27] Whitehead, Essays in Science and Philosophy 157 (1947).

If it be considered how seldom the individual citizen may undertake to deflect the course of government, how deficient his political equipment may be, and how much injury to lawful interests, delay, bickering, and confusion may result from his interference, the wonder will be not that there is so little but that there is so much mobility of ideas assured to him by democratic law. Stupid or uninformed, malicious or bromidic, he can nevertheless express what he is pleased to call his judgment. He may even have the right to inculcate hatred of some portion of the citizenry, to crack the national unity, or to preach up evil. The governors, who cannot believe that they need his views, generally feel obliged to defend that right. This relation is so unlikely and so peculiar that it demands some higher sanction.

The explanation may be sought in the democratic maxim of "majority rule," *i.e.*, that governors are constitutionally bound to respect the adjudication of the ballot box. But majority rule does not explain enough. It may justify free discussion *before* the votes are cast and the decision recorded. A society that affords any constitutional right to criticize *after* the general opinion has congealed, *after* the statute has been enacted, and especially *after* a venture has been launched into the affairs of other nations must subscribe to something beyond majority rule. In its operations, something more than an irrevocable voting arithmetic is implicit. Its course describes certain basic assumptions concerning the nature of man and the nature of truth. But since no human society accords quite the same mobility after as before its attainment of decision, these basic assumptions can hardly be deemed absolute or

self-evident. They are real enough in visible daily consequences to pervade democratic life with their quality.
These assumptions will be explicated in Part III of this
chapter; here it is important to observe that they are by no
means universally held, and that such acceptance as they
have remains precarious.

Movement of State Process. It is customary to regard
the Constitution following Aristotle and Polybius as a fu-
sion of types of polity, or following Locke and Montes-
quieu as a plan for division of functions, or following the
classical republicans [28] as a system of checks and balances,
or following Marx and Beard as an economic implement.
But whatever else the Constitution may be, it is unmistak-
ably a regulator of mobility in lawmaking. Certainly that
function has pervaded American theory ever since the au-
thors of the Massachusetts Body of Liberties declared " our
dutie and desire is to do nothing suddainlie which fundamentally concerne us." Each branch of government has
been shaped and reshaped to this policy, submitting to conceived restraints upon its rate of action.

So viewed, the judicial process acquires a new intelligi-
bility. All the carefully devised tenets of procedure, the
gray minutiae that have plagued lawyers and litigants down
the centuries, make their contribution toward the controlled flow of judicial action. Each requirement of notice, each formula for pleading or proffer, operates as a
moving element in the juridic rheostat and must justify its
continued existence by the effectuality of the current.

[28] Fink, The Classical Republicans: An Essay in the Recovery of a Pattern of Thought in Seventeenth Century England (1945). The same emphasis may be found, a century earlier, in Thomas More's Utopia.

Courts have always had to hesitate and stand still, move slowly or race forward as the composite procedural regulator permits, and their general pace of disposition has proved strikingly uniform. Technological advance may have fevered the balance of our topic, but the tempo of judicial process has hardly accelerated since the days of Gaius. For whatever of expedition was gained during the nineteenth century served only to offset earlier losses. In short, the inference is tempting that, granted temporary fluctuations, the speed of judicial movement continues fairly constant.

The Bill of Rights presents a notably fresh appearance when seen under the aspect of mobility. One perceives with new lucidity that many provisions of the Bill seek merely to brake the tempo of official action. They require government only to respect the forms and to proceed continently. The individual citizen obtains very few assurances that are even purportedly substantive; and, when these are challenged with force, he must generally appeal for the intervention of a court. Once he is in court, all the solemn charters of history can warrant him nothing more than a single incantative phrase: " due process of law." When judges prove fatuous, witnesses forgetful, advocates inept, or appellate tribunals myopic, there is no remedy in the books. Due process of law is the ultimate elixir, and, if it fails, everything fails. The Constitution does not confer perspicacity or guarantee infallible judgments. It promises the defendant a trial by his peers; to one who knows himself, this may be meager comfort. Why then is due process prized so highly?

Now, it is manifest that no legal system can claim a monopoly of the accepted attributes of due process. Notice to a defendant, opportunity for hearing and production of evidence, advice of counsel, application of presumptively known rules of law have been and are familiar phenomena not only of democracies, but also of the more efficient caste states and despotic empires.[29] Every kind of polity has a pragmatic need for due process, simply because it is a condition *sine qua non* of the lasting efficacy of every variety of law. To hang people without trial is to run the risk of hanging sheep for goats, and the tighter the despotism, the subtler the process of sorting out the species. Whenever the particular regulation under enforcement has had some large economic application, due process has offered the only safeguard against costly governmental error. It is the single technique by which a piece of substantively oppressive legislation can attain some measure of permanence. It will not long be ignored with impunity.

Apparently, then, the specifically democratic function of due process would emerge in those exceptional cases where the governors' fear or greed has blinded them to their own interest, or where hysteria has aroused the threat of mob savagery. In such instances men are apt to consider the denial of trial as the highest injury that may be in-

---

[29] We have Tacitus' testimony that the administration of Roman justice even under Tiberius (at least until the ascendancy of Sejanus) was characterized by fairness and integrity. Annals IV. vi. When degeneration did become manifest, it took the familiar form of literal legalism. For example, on Sejanus' fall, when it was desired to execute his wholly innocent little daughter, no precedent existing for the capital punishment of a virgin, she was violated by the executioner before being strangled. Annals V. ix. In the Middle Ages, some of whose inquisitorial practices cause us to shudder, serious efforts were made to rationalize and temper the steps in criminal proceedings. Ullmann, "Some Medieval Principles of Criminal Procedure," 59 Jurid. Rev. 1 (1947).

flicted on a citizen and to eulogize the writ of habeas corpus. But of what avail is the right to a trial if judges and juries are so tragically fallible? How can due process be the ultimate repository of the liberties of democratic man if, after the intricate machinery has turned and rolled, the end product may prove to be the electrocution of Sacco and Vanzetti? [30]

Here again juridic movement fails to present its own sanction. Though due process be the foundation of individual rights, it too requires an enduring bedrock on which to rest. There are presuppositions involved concerning the nature of man and truth, which confer on mobility its functional pre-eminence. Without those presuppositions, while due process could still infuse government with a certain rationality and purposiveness, the Bill of Rights would read like a skilled essay in irony.

Critique of Mobility. The foregoing exposition is obviously fragmentary, for we have assembled our data without expressly eliminating negative instances. Such a procedure imposes severe qualifications on the drawing of logically valid inferences; though it may illustrate the value and range of mobility, it does not begin to exhaust the concept. [31] Yet if allowance is made for the margin of error incident to a study of large scope, the procedure may at

---

[30] On May 21, 1947, a Greenville, South Carolina, jury acquitted twenty-eight white cabdrivers who, according to the statements of twenty-six of them made at the time of their arrest, had forced their way into the local jail, seized a Negro named Willie Earle, tortured and killed him. It is not clear whether the caliber of the jury or the weakness of the prosecution's presentation was responsible for this miscarriage. *See* Rebecca West, "Opera in Greenville," 23 The New Yorker 17, p. 31 (June 14, 1947), a valuable sociological document.

[31] To exhaust the concept, it would be necessary to divorce it from human experience, which is inexhaustible.

least carry persuasion. All reasoning is essentially a process of sampling, and inferences will be tenable in proportion to the representativeness of the samples. The data considered above are sufficiently numerous, broad in their sweep, and continuous in the temporal dimension to implant a sense of confidence. Even though our inferences should be confined to these data only, without pretense of wider applicability they might prove valuable enough.

At this date it is scarcely needful to deny that mobility in the law can be resolved to an exclusively economic formulation. That men do not act like mere economic automata is now widely recognized. Even when they attempt to guide themselves by economic signposts only, they often blunder, exacerbating the ills that they seek to cure. In fact, no analysis of human affairs can be quite complete that does not reckon with men's stubborn obtuseness. The riddle will not have a purely economic answer if only because " the Sphinx stands for stupidity." [32] It stands also for the many irrational drives that lend color and power to human undertakings.

Thus the concept of mobility is partially submerged in the universal inconclusive flux. There is an inadvertence, a nonpurposiveness, befogging the subject from the outset. The only way we can achieve factitiously sharp outlines is to succumb to one of the three dramatic illusions of our day; that is, *the illusion of the tableau, the illusion of*

[32] Dio Chrysostom, Tenth Discourse 32 (Loeb's trans. 1932), I, 441. The reported riddle of the Sphinx (what walks on four legs in the morning, etc.) was so transparent that it must have been meant ironically in sophisticated Hellas. The Sphinx did finally despair and commit suicide, not because the childish riddle was solved, but because a Hellenic hero and prince had answered it in all seriousness.

the epilogue, or *the illusion of the second-act curtain.*[33]

The illusion of the " tableau " is that which possesses uninformed or complacent observers. They believe that freedom resides in the present forms of law, which are all that they respect. They see the legal scene as a frozen pose and forget that Faust's penalty was incurred because he finally admitted himself contented with things as they are.

The second illusion arises out of a nostalgia for past achievements, to which current struggles seem like a mere " epilogue." Its victims believe that freedom resides in past forms, but this belief is so deeply impregnated with archaism that they see the past only as they would prefer it to have been. Distrustful of the adaptations in contemporary law, they forget that the techniques of the past are probably even less suited to current much less future needs.

Most seductive of all is the illusion of the " second-act curtain," highly cherished by scholars and theoreticians. Its dupes see the realization of freedom in the next following stage of constitutional forms. The second-act curtain has been rung down; the solution of all antitheses is surely ahead in the third and final act. They choose to forget that this, too, their proximate future, will soon fade through the present into the past. The temporal flux is not to be stayed.

It is essential therefore that the analysis seek to escape these illusions of the time perspective. Remembering that history has many voices, each age must somehow catch its own intimations of mobility and must listen among innu-

---

[33] Francis Bacon would recognize these, though they do not conform to his " idols of the theatre."

merable sounds for the note of freedom which is its proper tonic. The rank variety of data forbids us to resort to an easy monism; the facts are not fungible enough to submit to simple summation. But they may prove to be integrable.

From the outset of our synopsis, the notion that law is a regulator of tempo kept recurring continually. This notion has been accompanied by a persistent antistrophe: the acceleration of mobility due to technological advance. These two factors appeared to combine and interact, each stimulating the other, until at some stage conditions created by technical progress began to hamper the legal mobility of things, titles, and men. Thus in almost every facet of the study, the data seemed to intimate a hypothesis of movement toward limits. There was always a point beyond which mobility would not be pushed without passing into its opposite.

This intimation of limits might have been anticipated: it comports so well with the two beneficent meanings of order in human apprehension. Order's chief virtues for our purposes are (1) functional, and (2) psychological. Functional order is the progressively skillful adaptation of components to wholes, of means to ends, of materials to constructs. A functional order can remain static only so long as the needs of its operation require; it is merely the temporarily satisfying application of known implements. The sudden perception of a novel or unfamiliar order can be quite pleasurable when its association is functional, *i.e.,* manipulative. But order has a polar, psychological purpose: it denotes the accustomed, the habitual, the armchair in its usual place, and thus it carries rich overtones of ease and serenity.[34] Both these aspects of order are always subject to the interruptions and intrusions of chance. Chance subverts the best of functional adaptations and disarrays the patterns of comfortable habits. The only effective way to preserve order is therefore to allow for progress in functional relations, to apportion adequately the satisfactions of habit, and to leave a certain marginal looseness for the impact of the unforeseen. All this complex operation is assigned to the legal mechanism: by fixing and adjusting the tempo of movement, the law attempts to compromise functional with psychic order.

One of its devices in the process of adjustment is a tenure system, a congeries of rules governing relations among persons concerning things and titles. The tenure system both modifies and reacts to the rate of mobility. In disparate circumstances the very same system may be a useful implement or an intolerable obstacle. No single doctrine of property appears able to integrate freedom with order under all circumstances, because the principles of their own evolution do not inhere in the rules of tenure.

The analysis must therefore extricate itself from entanglement in devices, implements, and means which derive coloration from the ends they may serve or hinder; it must return to elements. At the beginning, mobility was viewed in an anthropocentric focus, and it has refused to conform to any other. The mobility under study is a human power, legal mobility a conceived marshaling of human power. The motif that ran through all manifestations of mobility

[34] An eloquent exposition of the beauties of this kind of order is contained in Ischomachus' lecture to his wife, as reported by Xenophon. Oeconomicus VIII. 3–23 (Loeb's trans. 1923), 429–39. It would have been fascinating to watch Mrs. Ischomachus' expression.

has been its significance for men. The tempo imposed by law proved suitable in so far as it suited men; to reckon its significance in other terms is to reckon without one's host.

Now, it is clear that the account of legal mobility contained no exposition of the qualitative human factor as influenced by law. Fixing on that factor, the inquiry may now advance its decisive question: If in the jurisprudence of freedom man is the measure of all things, with what shall man be measured? Perhaps, as suggested in the discussion of movement of ideas and of state process, he is to be measured by certain implicit presuppositions concerning his nature, the meaning of truth, and the role of law. These would furnish the measures and norms for an understanding of legal freedom.

Why, in fine, have the data of mobility appeared so suspenseful, so inconclusive? Why, like a broken weather vane, did they revolve but not point? There is a revealing clue in one of Baruch Spinoza's geometric propositions:

" If men were born free they would form no conception of good and evil as long as they were free." [35]

Our difficulty is that we have been studying movement in terms of *rate* without attending to *direction*. Tempo derives its worth from destination, and mobility alone tells nothing of this. The ultimate values of freedom must be measured by a standard that freedom cannot supply. Thus far, the account of juridic mobility was ordained to inconclusiveness, because criteria that might tell us when mobility is a good and when it is not must be searched for elsewhere. Absolute freedom is an amoral concept.

[35] Ethics, IV, prop. LXVIII.

III. *The Spirit of the Laws*

One of the enduring insights of Hellenic science was that the qualities of the citizen are relative to the type of state constitution under which he lives. Of course, this could not mean that the assumptions of a particular polity necessarily applied to all or any one of its citizens taken as individuals: Plato and Aristotle, like ourselves, were quite able to observe the mingled streaks of tyranny, oligarchy, monarchy, and mob rule in their acquaintances. It must mean rather that the constitution and laws presuppose certain general human traits, on whose reality and reliability they stake their success. The laws of a democratic society, for example, reveal the assumed attributes of a free man. Supplying as they do the theoretical sanctions of the law, these attributes are anterior to it in the order of logic; in practice, they should emerge from the operations of law as consequences and corollaries, for a free order can build the conditions of its own continuance and survival.[36]

Shifting Estimates. It is customary to charge eighteenth-century libertarians with a romantically exalted appraisal of man. The natural rights of the citizen were believed to be grounded upon faith in inherent human capacities. Man, the acme of rationality, would follow the truth as soon as he could see it, would accept the path of civic virtue once it was disclosed. Truth possessed some supernal

[36] Of course, hungry men are not free men. Anyone who has ever been hungry or sick knows what selfishness, irascibility, and indifference to the cares of others feel like. But it is illusory to expect that freedom can be equated with the full belly. The Strasbourg goose is more assiduously fed than any other creature — only to wind up as a *pâté*. Minimal economic provisions are a *condition* of freedom: with them, we are able to begin the real search.

magic, which upon the ripping down of feudal blinds could not be resisted. Free expression was indispensable to learning the truth; virtuous and rational men must hold it absolute and beyond the interference of government. They would transcend even class interests and group affiliations in their susceptibility to truth.

If this was the eighteenth-century view of man and of free expression, the theory has executed a remarkable *volte-face*. Leading twentieth-century libertarians have jettisoned the old admiration for man and for the magic of truth. They see humanity in history's glass, darkly. In apprehension man appears to resemble a god rather less than a perplexed and somewhat pathetic mole. The light of truth (whatever that may be) only dazzles him, and drives him back to the underground chambers of his irrationality. When he fails to follow his selfish class interests, it is only because he is too dull to decipher them. In this view, freedom of expression is precious and must be preserved, not because of man's capacities, but because of his congenital incapacities. For if all men are created esurient and myopic, and if truth is hopelessly subjective, no man's opinion is entitled to claim a monopoly of the market. There must be " free competition " even in the sale of shoddy ideational merchandise — perhaps the customers will somehow hit upon a passable parcel. Not the sight of truth but a profound skepticism makes men free.

However this antithesis between optimistic faith and cynical disbelief may serve to clarify the postulates of our concept, it is historically inaccurate. The statesmen of the eighteenth century were not so naïve as they have been made out. If we may, for purposes of rough summary, classify them into Jeffersonians and Hamiltonians, then obviously the latter entertained no roseate expectations concerning the citizen's rationality and virtue. In fact, the structure of government was most carefully designed by them to guard against popular impulse and viciousness. And what of the former, the Jeffersonians? Did they too not draw their philosophy from a want of confidence? While Hamilton distrusted men when armed with the power of the ballot, Jefferson distrusted them when armed with the power of government, and buttressed his constitutional fortress with that distrust. Proclaiming apparently contradictory creeds, these two progenitors of American state theory agreed that the existence of a free society could not be risked upon mere human susceptibility to the true. Men could not be trusted to obey light in the manner of eighteenth-century sundials, or of our photoelectric cells.

The democratic view appears to subsist somewhere between a fanatical optimism and pessimistic despair. Excess of optimism can lead only to the disappointment, bitterness, and rage that rejected zealots have exhibited in every age; and, at the other extreme, if all opinions are to be judged equally unworthy of trust, everlasting social debate is not worth its price in waste motion. Thus, expecting either too much or too little seems to end in the cult of compulsion. To save the republic, Hamilton must disregard his assumptions and accept the outcome of the ballot (as he did), Jefferson must disregard his and make use of the powers of government (as he did), and the " free competitive market " of ideas must have an increased number of discerning customers. In short, free expression will not be sanctioned by extreme estimates of human capacity or incapacity. Litmus, which responds accurately and immediately, has no analogue in the postulates of freedom.

Quality of Will. As legal systems mature they tend to rely increasingly on willing attitudes and dependable collaboration. The law's genesis is so closely associated with human aggressiveness and lust that the extent of this dependence may be easily overlooked. Yet, even in despotic states, a mature legal order must assume that judges and juries will exemplify some modicum of honor and integrity, that the tyrant's ordinance will in fact become the law of the specific case, and that despite the monumental aggregate of perjury in the halls of justice a remnant can be found of men who will swear to their own hurt. If there is no such thing as a righteous judge, it is necessary that the imaginations of the disputants supply one.

These assumptions are common to mature orders, whether democratic or despotic; they represent the keystone of the legal arch. Citizens and subjects accept the rule of law in the obdurate faith that the bench, the jury box, and the witness stand exercise a cathartic influence on the familiar impurities of their neighbors. There is a firm presumption that, at least *within the hierarchy of adjudication*, men generally intend to fulfill their duties, that subject to the restraints of positive legislation they purpose well toward their neighbors, and that they possess sufficient rational equipment to effectuate these desirable impulses. A decision or a verdict is law because of the force of this faith.

It is a prime postulate of free expression that this presumption of good intentions (a summary phrase to be elaborated below) may be extended to embrace the *entire citi-*

zenry — although, of course, in a somewhat diminished degree, for outside the courts speech is not so often equivalent to action. The postulate runs (1) that speakers with good intentions exceed in their influence those with evil intentions, (2) that the citizen audience has sufficiently good intentions of its own to desire the better persuasion, (3) that speaker and audience are rationally capable of discriminating between better and worse, and (4) that men have sufficient volitional freedom to follow the recognized good in the preponderance of instances.

Free expression serves to reduce the inner grudge against society, the subconscious resentment of monotony and discipline, the bitterness of the unfulfilled. By doing so, it may strengthen a latent desire to find working compromises, to tolerate and even protect the opposition; and it may foster the hope to be approved for one's own unique individuality. But these beneficences depend wholly upon the soundness of the fourfold postulate concerning volitional quality. They are inaccessible where evil intentions characterize the majority of speakers and auditors, or where reason has abdicated its claims (they would likewise be beyond reach in the hands of that ancient straw man — materialistic determinism).

As a pragmatic matter these assumptions center about the quality of the citizen auditor. The speakers of a society will generally arise from seats in the audience; though rather more articulate, they will presumably resemble the occupants of adjoining seats. Thus the rationality and ethical motivation of one may be expected to vary roughly with the same traits in the other. And since, in a democratic society, the final adjudication of values will reside not in the speaker but in the audience, the postulate of quality acquires an exceedingly wide compass. Free, democratic expression presupposes reasoned good will in a mass preponderance of the citizenry. This postulate is a bold one, particularly for an institution created — as the law was — in order to muzzle wolves; but then if men are never quite so good as our hopes for them, they are never so bad as our phantasms of despair.

Notions of Truth. That free expression assumes a fallibilistic and pluralistic understanding of truth seems rather obvious to current theory. The intellectual climate of liberty is now quite temperate, and it tends to forget its former zealous heat. Scorn is heaped on the absolutes of the past, and respect is reserved for propositions that openly concede their own subjectivity. Thus the principle that asks least by way of belief is credited most, and that which claims too much is simply spurned. But while it is true that most propositions are trustworthy only when intricately relative qualifications are annexed to them, a very few others may be acted upon quite absolutely. These latter are broad enough to fill their allotted cosmos.

To illustrate: The proposition that men are not distinguishable in the privileges of citizenship on any ground of religious belief may become absolute to a particular constitutional structure. The structure remains, of course, relative to its time, place, and tradition. Such a proposition may therefore be deemed *limited* or *finite;* that is to say, absolute within its frame of reference because wholly adequate in all the aspects of interest operative in that particular frame. Freedom of expression postulates some such finite notion of absolute principles. Its great and pious service is the elucidation of values; by that token its concern must be with finitude, from which all cognizable values flow.[37]   But in an era of agnostic relativism, theorists should recall that some finites, like the terrestrial globe, are without boundaries.   Relative as they may be *sub specie aeternitatis*, they are nevertheless absolute in the complex of human decision and action.   They become true and may later become false, as they are validated or invalidated in the life of the ethos.   To call them eternally absolute is to ignore the chamber that they occupy; to judge them merely relative is to overlook the completeness with which they fill it.   Finite truths, *e.g.*, that a man should not be judge in his own cause, are the operative implements of a working freedom.

The Human Rhythm.   At this stage the imputed image of the free man begins to emerge.   He appears capable of rational conviction, ethical impulsion, and perception of significant finite truths.   On the other hand, he seems perilously fallible in both judgment and moral discernment. His *immediate* responses to the issues of social existence are seldom astute or reliable, much less automatically accurate. The quality, therefore, of the free man would remain inchoate and the sanctions of popular government equivocal, were it not for a further determinant; to wit, the active influence of legal technique.

The law exercises its affective function by adjusting the tempo of motion to the human rhythm.   Ideas and state process in movement present democratic man with critical occasions for intellectual and imaginative response.   The

[37] "The superstitious awe of infinitude has been the bane of philosophy."   Whitehead, Essays in Science and Philosophy 103 (1947).

juristic postulate is that, if such movement is held to an ideally suitable rate, the response will prove as excellent as men's congenital limitations permit. The legal machinery thus stakes its success on the efficacy of deliberation; whether by means of division of governmental powers or association of several individuals in a single decision, or requirement of delays in the progress of a lawsuit, it enforces deliberation as the optimum condition of right action. It exacts an appeal from Philip drunk to Philip sober, from childish impulse to mature emotion, from first impression to final wisdom. It retards in order to perfect.

Deliberation, the law assumes, will compel a judge or administrator to give himself reasons for his action and to weigh their value. To make certain that he does so, the established techniques usually require him to disclose his formalized reasons to others, for (as the Gemara blandly remarks) " if it were not permitted to judge him, how could he judge? " [38] Thus the law insists not only that a judge have time for deliberation but also that he indicate the actual exploitation of his opportunity. In this sense, even a very wise judicial or administrative decision uttered without assignment of reasons may appear presumptuous and intellectually suspect. Here then is the explanation for the strangely constant tempo of judicial process down the centuries: the interval requisite for maturing the mental and emotional reactions of men remains stable in a world where almost everything else accelerates. Fortunately, however, since official deliberation must ultimately end in decision

[38] This comment relates to an incisive provision of the Mishnah — a king, being exempt from being judged, is not permitted to act as judge. Rodkinson, Babylonian Talmud, vols. 7 and 8 (XV and XVI), c. 2, 44 (1918).

and action, social pressures have tended to keep the waiting periods within tolerable limits, to compel the occasional improvisation of more energetic procedures, and to restrict the use of injunctive delay in labor disputes. Of course, there still remain for the entertainment of posterity such anomalies as the senatorial filibuster. But a filibuster or an abuse of *liberum veto* (in the Council of the United Nations) is not deliberation; it is rather the refusal to deliberate. The objective in law is that men realize their uncertain best the only way they can — by taking thought to themselves.

Free expression in the form of public discussion compels the general citizenry to deliberate over issues, just as the necessity of assigning reasons compels the judge. The many competitive voices, in their sometimes raucous debate, serve to retard the crystallization of final judgment — presenting not only various conflicting views of the matter but, more important, the challenge to reflect, to analyze, and to assume a sober attitude. These outer voices have their echoes within, and every public contention evokes some private assent or rebuttal. It is not enough for those on the rostrum to look to their case; their scattered partisans are visited with the same kind of burden. Democratic decisions are notoriously tardy; doubtless they are all too often mistaken. But free discussion and deliberation are designed to diminish the empire of unreason and to give rationality whatever function it is able to fulfill in human enterprises.

The Sense of Injustice. We have noted the polyphonic motifs that together make up the melody of juristic freedom, and we have seen how legal technique, like a metronome, serves to regulate their rhythm. Certainly to any-one who, being ignorant of the aspirations of a democratic polity, is deaf to this melody the visible motions of free men must seem strange if not a little mad. The dance would look grotesque without the tune. Yet we too who have acquired some familiarity with this composite strain may properly wonder whether men do in fact dance to it. An ideal pattern is persuasive enough for hypothetical con-structs and for the illumination of premises, but when it makes bold to interpret practical affairs it must survive the tests of daily life. What reason have we to believe that the postulated free man actually corresponds, in rationality and good intention, to his living counterparts? Is the pat-tern that we have traced merely an overweening compli-ment which democratic man has elected to pay himself; is there any earnest whatever that these attributes may be predicable of human beings in fact as well as in theory?

That earnest is to be found in the sense of injustice, the operative instrument through which freedom builds its moral values and its consequent claims on the law. The sense of injustice (which was rather fully described in the chapter on " Justice and Power ") is that indissociable blend of reason and empathy in the human endowment by means of which men are enabled to detect, to resist, and to repel a threatened wrong. Functionally it manifests itself in an imagined interchange so that, within the limits of subjective relevance, an unjust attack on another is identi-fied as a species of personal jeopardy. This interchange brings emotional and glandular reactions, which enable men to resist assault. Thus the sense of injustice equips a human being to increase progressively the ambit of his own

career and to survive and grow in an expanding community of experience. Without it, he is locked in the walls of
his psychic cell; with it he can become a spiritual congener.

When, therefore, legal freedom postulates a preponderance of good intentions, the sense of injustice can accord
nerve and muscle to that assumption — at least so far as the
men of the given polity have developed their capacity of
interchange. To that extent they will defend for others
whatever they recognize as needful to themselves, and if
they have learned to prize their own legal mobility their
neighbors' too will remain secure. Even without a cultivated sense of injustice, human beings may be willing to
risk death for their own freedom, for to become unfree is
to lose power, to atrophy, to die in part. But only the mysterious interchange that informs the sense of injustice can
spur men to accept that supreme risk for the freedom of
others or enable them to protect the advocacy of the very
thoughts which they detest. " The people," it is said,
" must fight for the law as for city-walls "; [39] they may indeed fight for the law if its postulates find so effective a
complement in themselves.

It is important to observe that the mere declaration of
the postulates of free expression is a creative summons to
the sense of injustice. Although the pattern of the democratic man frequently appears all too flattering when set
against the activities and pursuits of the market place, yet
some rudimentary sense of injustice must be discoverable
before that pattern could even be conceived; and if, like
the stars by day, it seems unnoticed and neglected, it is
nonetheless real and refulgent. The very assertion of a

[39] Heraclitus, *apud* Diogenes Laërtius IX. i (Loeb's trans. 1931), II, 409.

right of free expression, though hypocritical, indicates that the sense of injustice has stirred. But, of course, that is not enough; this kind of light remains incomplete until it joins with fire, until empathy has marshaled its forces into the ranks of rational perception. The reign of freedom is therefore designed for peoples who are ready to resent and repel injustice, and who would never deserve Archilochus' reproach: " You have no gall to burn your liver! " [40]

We have already seen that the sense of injustice (obscured though it may be by positive influences) is part of man's native capacity, that it is an operative factor in the law, and that it can improve and mature. Surely if freedom is the morally colorless concept we have judged it to be, only when infiltrated by such a dye can it acquire merit and survival value. The democratic man confers dignity on freedom to the degree that his sense of injustice has been refined and cultivated. Truth, it had to be conceded, has no inevitable or automatic appeal for him; on the contrary, he may be so drawn to falsehood and vice that society considers him irredeemable and excludes him from its shores, or shuts him away, or hangs him by the neck. These courses are obnoxious to a society that aspires to freedom, because they are tokens of its own shortcomings; and it will accordingly seek to reduce the causes of such abandonments. But, more important, it must endeavor to develop the sense of injustice in the redeemable mass of its citizens. This is its ultimate and only hope. Unless the sense of injustice can be cultivated in daily use, unless habits of justice can be *learned*, freedom is only an idle and deceptive figment. Thus the profound question for juris-

[40] A fragment quoted by Jaeger, 1 Paideia 124 (2d ed. 1945).

prudence is: How can the law itself contribute to education of the sense of injustice? Is it possible to discover within the principles and operations of law some sort of subtly effectual mentor?

IV. " *That Most Excellent Leading-String of the Law* " [41]

Pedagogic Criticisms. No one can fairly expect a teacher to practice precisely what he teaches, but if the gap between precept and example spreads too wide it alienates and embitters the students. The law's value in the education of citizens can be nullified by a regime of oppression, unjust privilege, or judicial corruption. Where the legal system serves only as an arm of caste power, its educational pretensions will meet the scorn they deserve. Thus, some forty years ago, when Petrazhitsky [42] (eminent Polish-Russian theorist) urged that the law could serve a lofty pedagogic purpose, Leo Tolstoy dismissed this claim as " impudence," " stupidity," and " defiance of common sense " [43] — because Petrazhitsky taught and wrote within the last degenerate period of czarist despotism. The legal operations of that period were hardly suited to inculcate

[41] Plato, Laws 645A (Loeb's trans. 1926), I, 69.

[42] The most adequate exposés of Petrazhitsky in English are Babb, "Petrazhitskii — Science of Legal Policy and Theory of Law," 17 Bost. U. L. Rev. 793 (1937), and the same author's "Petrazhitskii: Theory of Law," 18 *id.* at 511 (1938). There are four informative articles on Petrazhitsky in Interpretations of Modern Legal Philosophies: Essays in Honor of Roscoe Pound (1947). Valuable analyses are those of Alexandre Grouber, "Une Théorie psychologique du droit," 10 Revue trimestrielle de droit civil 531, 556, *et seq.* (France, 1911), and Max Laserson, "Russische Rechtsphilosophie," 26 Archiv für Rechts-und-Wirtschaftsphilosophie 289, 324-36 (Germany, 1933).

[43] Quoted, Laserson, Russia and the Western World 123 (1945).

civic virtue. Unless, therefore, a jural system exhibits integrity and responsibility, it cannot assume the role of a helpful tutor.

Moreover, as silk purses do not result from the processing of sows' ears, law alone will not metamorphose the ethos in which it operates. Good laws are laws congruent to the needs of people in a given time and place; good order is such order as they may then and there require and the standard of freedom must be such that they may enjoy it without sinking into social chaos. A code of laws, Plato and Isocrates rightly insisted, is not like a liberty cap for whoever may choose to don it. The ethos must be made ready, and for the purposes of that training law is only one instructor in a numerous faculty of institutional influences. Hence it is that proposed great leaps of reform have so often to be divided into short and tedious hops suitable to the stature of the particular folk.

These are commonplace admonitions which the pedagogy of the law can cheerfully digest. They serve merely to caution against excessive claims and quixotic enterprises. There are, however, certain other considerations that might seem so impassable as to bar the law from any educational role whatever. The more fundamental criticisms are:

1. That legal process lacks the individualization necessary to sound pedagogy. To this the law may reply that it does within limits individualize its techniques; that excessive individualization as among cases and persons is undesirable in a tightly knit industrial economy; that the claim to individualized desert must be restricted by the competing claim to equality before the law; and that its tenets of

moral responsibility would be nullified by a wholly clinical *tout comprendre, tout pardonner*.

2. That legal rules have such working prestige that they tend to supplant moral rules and thus to consecrate the ethics of the market place. On this score the law must concede that the ethical individual does and should surpass its requirements and that its history includes such abominations as legalized servitude. It is able, however, to erect a standard better than that of the Philistines, and if it must fall short of the truly righteous who do not need correction it can improve us, the overwhelming majority who do.

3. That law is always held back by the constraints of positive tradition, fine distinction, and undue respect for precedent. To this the law may file its demurrer: if it is to furnish useful guidance, it must teach in terms of a given perspective, it must enact rules refined enough to match the complexities of human affairs, it must urge that precedent which assumes reliance should not be needlessly ignored. (Having won this point, the law discovers an uneasy feeling of partial guilt.)

4. That law is an instrument of force for the maintenance of the *status quo*. This is as true as the proposition that law is an instrument of force for amelioration or deterioration of the *status quo*, for progress or reaction. The given does enjoy a strong presumption of validity, but that presumption appears outside as well as inside the scope of the law. Although law concededly resorts to force when persuasion will not succeed, the fate of any legal system depends upon persuasion's success in the preponderance of cases. As long as society needs to exert some species of

compulsion, law can at least present a paradigm of persuasion's progressive encroachment on the areas of force.

5. That law deals with external actions only and does not consider their subjective quality. This fallacy drawn from Kant has been frequently repeated [44] — even by those whose technical knowledge should have guarded against a layman's facile dichotomy. The view attributed to Kant was mistaken in that superlative degree which only a priori speculation ever attains. The fact is that law is everlastingly concerned with subjective states, with motives, purposes, and intents; the jural value of almost any overt act depends upon ascertainment of its subjective concomitants. From criminal law to taxation, from testamentary construction to the formation of contracts, the motive or intent is constantly under critical inquiry. Granted that the law must often infer the intent from objective indicia, is this not the common necessity of all social intercourse? Granted that (*e.g.*, in cases of driving at excessive speed) the law will sometimes attach its sanctions disregarding some commendable idiosyncratic motive, is this policy not generally confined to acts which have consequences light for the actor but potentially heavy for others? A sensitive morality would insist, as the law does, on the superior claim of the passive many in such secondary transactions. Moreover, in terms of pedagogic technique, the law may reasonably anticipate that its very refusal to receive esoteric excuses may act as an effectual deterrent. And when it seeks

[44] This view attributed to Kant had been anticipated by Lucas de Penna at least. Ullmann, The Medieval Idea of Law as Represented by Lucas de Penna 61 (1946). Kant's dichotomy appeared in his "Introduction to the Metaphysic of Morals" and in his Preface to the Metaphysical Elements of Ethics. *See* distinction made in Pound, The Task of Law, lecture III (1944), and Weiss, Nature and Man 66 (1947).

to construct this or any other deterrent, the law again evinces its preoccupation with states of mind.

These several criticisms do not then disqualify (though they should serve to chasten) our mentor. Despite them, there survives the obsessive vision of Hebraic and Hellenic thinkers that law shall become a lamp to the feet and a light to the path. This vision was the final radiance in Plato's sunset and it has recently shone anew through the writings of Petrazhitsky. It is the reasoned assurance that the spirit of the laws can in time suffuse the laws of the spirit.

Heteronomy. Law's pedagogy begins with the level of what may be called " imposed " order. On this level the legal system reacts to wrongful conduct by exercising some species of constraint such as imprisonment, execution, imposition of fine or penalty, enforcement of restitution or specific performance. Compulsion, actual or threatened, is used in order to induce the desired behavior, and society's advantage over the individual consists primarily in the superiority of its organized force. The purposes of education on this level are illustrated by the evolutionary schema of criminal law.

Within little more than a single millennium the characteristics of criminal law may pass through seven stages of progressive development. These are:

a) Primitive retaliation by an individual or clan, continuing until religious sanctity attaches to the code of law and sacrilegious guilt to the offender;

b) Attribution of revenge or retribution to the will of the divinity, making the offender an outcast whom it is obligatory to exclude or kill (thus the mark of Cain was designed not to brand him as a murderer but to reduce his

punishment to mere exclusion from any organized group
— " lest any finding him should smite him "),[45] such practices proving costly in blood as society coalesced;

c) Composition in kind (eye for eye,[46] etc.) or in
money at officially published rates paid to the injured person or to his tribe,[47] with a diminishing option in the offender to offer and in the injured to accept pecuniary
satisfaction;

d) Punishment as composition with the political sovereign, who, because of the loss of subject man power resulting from acts of violence, gradually assumes jurisdiction to
prosecute [48] and to collect fines (hence the criminal is said
to " pay his debt to society " or " to pay the price "), now
more generally viewed as an assertion of sovereign authority and supremacy;

e) Growing emphasis on deterrence by means of penal
example (de Penna, Beccaria, and Holmes rejected all

[45] Genesis 4.15.

[46] Solon introduced a clever refinement of this general rule: the penalty
for depriving a one-eyed man of his *single* eye was the loss of the offender's
two eyes.   Diogenes Laërtius, Solon I, 57 (Loeb's trans. 1925), I, 57.
Quaere: Suppose a one-eyed man deprives a two-eyed man of one eye?

[47] The contractual element in primitive submission to judgment is best
illustrated by the Njals Saga, Kocourek and Wigmore, Evolution of Law
Series, 1 Sources of Ancient and Primitive Law 122 (1915).   Traces thereof
long remained in the Roman action of sacramentum.   Buckland, A Text-
Book of Roman Law from Augustus to Justinian 610–16 (2d ed., 1932).
The progression in state authority is neatly illustrated by comparing The
Short Version of Iaroslav's Pravda (which restricted blood revenge to certain close relatives of the slain person), with The Expanded Version or
Pravda of Iaroslav's Sons (which abolished all blood revenge and required
composition in money in all cases).   Medieval Russian Laws 26, 35 (Vernad-
sky ed. 1947).

[48] Only in the late Middle Ages did western European criminal prose-
cutions gradually become free of the Roman " *subscriptio*," which had so
long made them a dangerous private enterprise.   The accuser, in the " *subscriptio*," had to undertake to suffer the same punishment if the accused
should not be convicted.   Unfortunately, the way out was found in the
notorious procedure of " *inquisitio*."   *See* Ullmann, " Some Medieval Principles of Criminal Procedure," 59 Jurid. Rev. 1 (1947).

other conceptions of punishment), the deterrence being addressed first to wrongs only, later to all kinds of social harms;

f) A philosophical or religious advocacy of punishment (in the " penitentiary "), as purification or penitence of which the wrongdoer cannot be justly deprived,[49] the focus beginning to fix on the wrongdoer as a salvageable subject rather than an outcast object;

g) The undertaking, whether sentimental or rational, to achieve reformation of the criminal by preparing him for a new existence of social usefulness.

These are the strata; they are not successive but cumulative. Though punishment is gradually guided to more rational purposes of deterrence or reformation, it does not slough off its primitive uses. It still satisfies the felt need for retaliation and affords release to the shock and rage of those who witness any act of violence. For when these inner acids of anger and vindictiveness begin to boil, they must find an outlet or they will corrode the sense of psychic security and eventually spill over on unoffending neighbors. The criminal law can move from force through honorable shame to persuasion; but in the process it must take more into account than the Ishmaels who may possibly be reclaimed.

The value of imposed order arises out of its direct relation to the sense of injustice. At every stage in the evolution of criminal law there is evidence of that persistent reciprocity between men which is rooted in their being equals; there is evidence of a peremptory demand for the imposi-

---

[49] Plato, Protagoras 324 and Gorgias 469, *et seq. See* Jaeger, 2 Paideia 135 (1943).

tion of individual desert. These rudimentary manifestations of the sense of injustice have been slowly improved and refined through the emerging influence of still another manifestation; *i.e.*, the insistence on human dignity. To teach men that the remedy for crime is in resort to law as opposed to self-help will avail only where law itself places a progressively greater stake on the realizable worth of human beings and thus acts consistently with its own admonitions.

The highest educational achievement of imposed order relates, however, not to criminals or their victims but to the whole of society. Society has been generally viewed as acting upon the criminal and prosecution has been regarded as a stimulus to some reaction on his part. This reaction is only one side of the learning process. Society, the stimulus, reacts in turn to the trial that it institutes and the punishment that it inflicts. It rarely identifies itself so completely with its state judicial system that it cannot criticize or feel revulsion when a miscarriage takes place. At times the brutality of criminal procedure has opened society's eyes to the existence of widespread maladjustments, and the revelation has been intensified by the thought that in a democracy the citizens are answerable for the doings of the law.

Under the American Constitution they are answerable to a peculiar degree. This responsibility arises from the historical relation between the Fourteenth Amendment and the original Bill of Rights, as construed by the Supreme Court. The Court holds that it cannot interfere with the criminal procedures of a state unless they offend some fundamental principle of justice, deeply rooted in the traditions and conscience of the whole people.[50] The public sense of injustice thus becomes a constitutional criterion. Its quality and sensitivity determine constitutional law: the basic rights of each human integer depend upon standards attained by a general mass. And if anyone suffers the loss of such rights, who but the callous many should be called to answer?

It is recorded that Willie Francis, convicted of murder, was placed in the electric chair, that the current was turned on but did not kill him,[51] and that the Supreme Court was petitioned under the Eighth and Fourteenth Amendments to forbid a second attempt at electrocution. The reports show that four justices could discover nothing " cruel or unusual " in a second execution, because forsooth cruelty was not intended by the state authorities. This extraordinary reasoning recalls the ancient comment of Bion that, though boys throw stones at frogs in sport, yet the frogs do not die in sport but in earnest.

Suppose, however, that a justice should feel horrified and enraged by the prospect of a second attempt at extermination under the authority of law. What then is his

[50] The development of this doctrine is described in Louisiana v. Resweber, 329 U. S. 459 (1947). A strong minority of the Court contends that state criminal procedures are subject to all constitutional requirements that affect federal criminal procedures, not only those requirements that involve the public conscience. Adamson v. California, 332 U. S. 46 (1947). The result in the case about to be discussed would probably have been the same under either view.

[51] Louisiana v. Resweber, *supra* note 50. The electrocutioner pulled down the switch and at the same time said "Goodbye Willie." Willie Francis' lips puffed out, he groaned, and his body squirmed and tensed; he jumped so that the chair rocked on the floor. The man in charge saw that Willie Francis was not dying and yelled for "more juice." The shout came back that "he was giving him all he had." Then Willie Francis cried: "Take it off. Let me breathe." And they took the hood from his eyes and unstrapped him. Affidavits of official chaplain and official witnesses, quoted *ibid.*, dissenting opinion, footnote 2.

course to be?   He may, by imaginative interchange, attribute his own revulsion to civilized men in general and insist that the Fourteenth Amendment forbids a reapplication of the current.   Such was the conviction of the four dissenting justices.   If, on the other hand, he is able to doubt that his personal feeling is shared by the mass of society, he may exercise one of three choices: (1) he may, on reflection, see fit to credit his fellow citizens with a sense of injustice as responsive as his own and add his deciding vote to the four dissents; (2) to the same purpose, he may see fit to invest the administration of justice with a duty of slightly surpassing and *pro tanto* educating the social conscience,[52] at least where the capital penalty is involved; or (3) declining to compliment either the citizenry or the educational ideal of law, he may cast his reluctant vote for noninterference with the determination of the state.   The third course was in fact chosen.   The second, " successful " execution ensued.   This time it was the law's estimate of its role in a free society that failed.

Success or failure of the law's pedagogic vocation is nowhere so important as in the area of imposed order.   Here executive and judicial action relate directly to men's physical being; consequently the object lessons presented are exceedingly clear and easy to digest.   If the public sense of injustice is assumed to be of high caliber, then legal procedure becomes a " leading-string " of understanding and strength and service on the trial jury offers a training

---

[52] *See* Gray, The Nature and Sources of the Law 285–90 (2d ed. 1921), where it is submitted that, in a case where there is nothing to guide the judge but notions of right and wrong, the judge should follow his own notions even though they differ with those of the community.

ground in republican ideals. It is therefore incumbent on judges to persist in advancing the standard of imposed order and to trust firmly in a concurrent rise of social response.

Strengthening Social Filaments. The turning point of imposed order arrived, as we have seen, when redress for injuries was no longer considered the private monopoly of the injured person or tribe. That change was significant because it heralded the gradual rise of a sovereign jural system and the emergence of state power. It had, however, an additional and very special meaning for the pedagogic function of democratic law. If every citizen could institute a prosecution on behalf of the injured against the wrongdoer, or if a formal representative of all citizens were charged with that duty, the whole population would become accustomed " as members of one body, to feel and resent one another's injuries." [53] Imposed order, as it laid the foundation for state authority, concomitantly introduced solidarity, responsibility, and dignity to the ways of men.

In modern states the analogous turning point consists in legislation for full employment and social security. The redress for private injuries suffered from poverty, old age, or unemployment has shifted from the individual to governmental organs, and for present purposes the prime value of that transition inheres in its inculcative capacity. Social legislation has translated the sympathy of imaginative interchange into daily work, bread, and confidence. The lessons of such legislation persist: security provisions, once

[53] Solon *apud* Plutarch, 83 (Langhorne ed. 1889).

introduced, are very quickly grasped as indestructible rights, for they accord so clearly with the public sense of injustice.

Even the most solicitous safeguards against economic hardship do not alone create democratic solidarity. Certain taught habits of self-discipline are equally necessary. The laws instill habits of control to the extent that they exhibit their own control of economic monopolies, of political or religious majorities, of the several arms of government, and finally of government as an operating whole. They impose order on the official instruments of order, define the ambit of official jurisdiction, and prescribe the channels of procedure. And where these purposes are pursued wisely, a democratic state may hold its liberties without surrender of efficiency or power. The doctrine is that, however one may grab, power and responsibility are tied in the same package; that if one reaches for responsibility he gets power as well; but if one reaches for power his hand will be cut on its blade.

Responsibility is most effectively taught by means of the device of review. The power requisite to governing in a dynamic era is generated by allowing officials to act first and account later — to the administrative superior, the supervisory court, the party caucus, or the electorate. It is through review that men learn to respect social authority and to measure its and their own fallibility. But just because review may follow long after the event, and may carry the condescending wisdom of hindsight, it can be a delicate and slippery instrument.

The dangers inherent in review's aposteriority become manifest in constitutional cases. Let us suppose that the elementary immunities of an accused have been violated by police officers or by the trial judge under circumstances which the Supreme Court (many weary months later) finds did not " prejudice " the fairness of the trial. In any such case, if the Court should reverse the conviction on the principle that violation of basic rights necessarily imports " prejudice," it risks penalizing society for some official's harmless mistake, immaterial to the outcome of the prosecution under review. If, on the other hand, it requires evidence of actual " prejudice " in the presented case, it slashes the shield not only of the accused but of all other citizens, and reduces an immunity intended for all (even for the innocent) to one reserved exclusively for those few who are eventually convicted by means of the pertinent violation. This is poor instruction indeed for both officer and citizen. It is most harmful when the vicious instance arises within *ipsos custodes*, the courts themselves.

The free citizen may rightly deduce from the processes of review that all men (rulers, generals, judges, priests, scientists, experts, and wise men alike) are created fallible. This inference teaches him, in the half light of his own perceptions, a certain dignity and responsibility, for though he is as fallible as they his errors are not so pretentious or costly. Free expression is indispensable to him if only to expose their mistakes and to prick their flatulence. His republican constitution teaches that every official decision may be wrong — not excepting the instant one, which, however, it is prudent to obey pending appeal. It teaches that even the wildest and most implausible opinion may some day be vindicated by acceptance. Senatorial and judicial robes are therefore much like the monarch's new robe in Hans Christian Andersen's tale: the moment the populace decides that there is no robe, there will be none. In such a relation, one may fairly ponder which is subject and which is king.

Edification. The specific lessons of law, on the higher level of civil order which we now consider, pertain seldom to substantive or content principles, for these will shift and change with the passage of time and the recognition of new demands. The lessons pertain rather to form, to human attitudes, and to the orientation of the citizen in the state. They are subtly and implicitly conveyed and are heard like overtones, almost indistinguishably.

a) Precision. The law follows the precedent of Adam, whose first recorded act was to give names to all living things.[54] It constitutes definitive categories to which happenings and relations are to be assigned. It trains the sense of injustice to rationalize its raw reactions, to analyze and understand before passing judgment, to discover conceptual order in the eternal flux. The drawing of lines thus acquires both an intellectual and a moral value.

b) Flexibility. Equity and administrative process teach that the law was made not merely for man, the species, but for individual men, and that syllogistic rules must at times be made to bend, lest they break. In the extreme case, these considerations may require final resort to a president's or governor's pardon.[55] There are instances in which law,

---

[54] This process was undoubtedly facilitated by the circumstance that it preceded the creation of Eve.

[55] The reader will hardly have forgotten the somewhat lurid facts of Queen v. Dudley, summarized on p. 29, note 18 *supra*. He should now be informed that the sentence of death imposed on the two seamen was commuted by the Crown to six months' imprisonment. Reporter's Note, 14 Q. B. D. at 288 (1884).

nurtured on reason, must demonstrate reason's inadequacy. But the pardon too is an act of law and in it law may be vindicated as flexible and compassionate.

c) Realism. A legal rule is vulnerable that will not attempt to operate through appearance upon substance. Eventually it will be battered by the persistent realities of economic and social existence. The law sets up forms that it challenges men to see through, to handle, and, where profitable, to replace. The lesson is not so much in the forms as in their manipulation.

d) Reciprocity. *Lex talionis* taught this doctrine in huts and forests; equity jurisprudence still insists on it. Through reciprocity in the law, men are led to respect the rights of others in an expanding community of interchange. Reciprocity has the pedagogic advantage of dramatic color: as when, Pliny recounts, a famous criminal trial of his day was interrupted in order that the prosecutor himself might be indicted, tried, convicted, and sentenced.[56]

e) Moderation. The legal system insinuates that a man may have his desire if he will only evince some considerate regard for the impact on others. It counsels tempered ambition and moderated pace. Even when permitting economic oppression, it endeavors to restrain extreme abuses, for its own existence depends upon temperance. There are times when men should not be moderate, and at such times the law can offset its customary gradualness by offering the procedure for revolution and new order.[57] In gen-

[56] Pliny, Letters III. ix (Loeb's trans. 1915), I, 227. Other colorful instances are mentioned in Boethius, Consolation of Philosophy II. vi (Loeb's trans. 1918), 207, *et seq.*

[57] Plato, Laws 770E.

eral, however, the legal system is averse to incontinence and roughshod ways; the contest it regulates is brutal enough but not without rules and reins. Where class struggles for mastery over class, the traits of law admonish compromise, self-control, and profitable generosity.

f) Projection. The appeal to conscience has been the dominant note of equity jurisprudence; law attempts a similar appeal by its emphasis on motive or purpose. That a privilege may be lost if maliciously exercised, that rights may be forfeited if abused — these are lectures in the obligatory art of interchange. By them the owner is warned to project himself beyond the walls of his selfishness and to learn that property is held in a reciprocal trust.

g) Solidarity. The sense of injustice calls for disinterestedness, which is opposed to both self-seeking (interestedness) and callous indifference (uninterestedness). The law seeks to exemplify disinterestedness in the ideal of the righteous judge. Of course, that ideal is only a figment; yet it has fired and exalted the imaginations of men through the millennia. The disinterested judge is seen as the sense of injustice personified and incarnate. He must exhibit what is human in men and nothing else, their generic without their individual qualities. In that sense, all litigants before him must be equal, because he is the institutional instrument of equality. He represents impersonality and therefore cannot respect persons. The judge is thus an emblem of democratic solidarity; his office is the symbol of the public conscience creating acts of justice. Even his limitations and imperfections, if they be honorable and candid, are tokens of solidarity, for they too are generic. The wholly righteous judge is a figure of myth, literally false but replete with the truth of aspiration and resolution.

Autonomy. This is the curriculum of democratic law. Its discipline is loose enough to leave room for the natural exuberance of human beings and for the kind of high adventure that transcends regulation. The law's instruction addresses itself not only to individual monads but likewise to groups, classes, and associations of every species. And the exemplar of this curriculum is the autonomous citizen; for legislation's utmost product is *man legislating for himself.*

He legislates for himself by choosing representatives to conduct the affairs of government, by active exertion in the shaping of their decisions, and by participation in craft, local, or regional enterprises that call for decentralized administration. These are the conspicuous autonomies, highly valued because hardly won.

Then there are the covert autonomies of the free citizen. He legislates for himself by appreciating the intentional value of jural situations, as his private sense of injustice becomes more and more immanent in the public conscience. The sense of injustice that contributes to the making of law inheres in him; it has its being and its sanction in his endowment. Legal order becomes his order; the rewards of compliance and the penalties of infraction are less outside than within. Law can prepare him for that acme of self-rule asserted by Aristotle [58] (and Xenocrates [59]): " I do of my own accord what some are constrained to do by their fear of the law " and depicted even more

---

[58] Diogenes Laërtius, Aristotle, V (Loeb's trans. 1925), I, 463.
[59] Cicero, De re publica I. ii (Loeb's trans. 1928), 17.

proudly by Aristippus: "Should all laws be repealed, we shall go on living as we do now." [60]

This is not the autonomy of a utopia. It holds no visionary hope that imposed order may "wither away" [61] or that wolves will learn to gambol with the lambs. Sick and vicious minds we shall always have with us, even in the future society of our best resolves. The program is more modest, more attainable. It allows for varying degrees of imperfection in all men, recognizes the indefinitely enduring need for some kind of imposed order, and acknowledges the influence of many other mentors in the school of society. But it does assure that the "leading-string" performs its work and that an order which draws so much shape and strength from internal sources can become increasingly voluntary.

Freedom, itself an amoral concept, has been accorded nobility in the ideal pattern of the democratic man. Law may so educate men as to make them not unworthy of that pattern. They may thus become free in the only sense accessible to social life; that is, subject to an order of their own fashioning. The order without partakes of the order within and is molded in its image. Mindful, moreover, of what is spontaneous and anarchic in man's nature, both orders must always remain loose and fit for play.

In "Justice and Power" it was found that *state* power attains its highest form when it is in synthesis with an order of humane justice. Now, at this platform in our present ascent, the same is seen to be true of that species of *indi-*

---

[60] Diogenes Laërtius, Aristippus II. 68 (Loeb's trans. 1925), 199.

[61] Engels forecast that under complete communism the state would "wither away." The rise and fall of the influence of this ideal are described objectively in Schlesinger, Soviet Legal Theory (1945).

vidual power which we call " freedom." The paths have met in affirmation. Justice is more than a philosopher's concept or distant goal; to the free man, it is a constant and familiar companion. " For common justice can determine private freedom, as a clear sky can tempt men to astronomy, or a peninsula persuade them to be sailors." [62]

[62] Auden, " In Time of War " in Collected Poetry 345 (1945).

SECURITY AND CHANGE

*The business is, to be able to make the Earth
move without a thousand inconveniences.*

— GALILEO, *Dialogue on the Two Chief Systems*

I. *The Elements*

HUMAN INSECURITY is a pervasive fact the philosophy
of law must learn to reckon with. The places where
a man has reason to feel insecure are land, sea, and air, and
the justifiably anxious hours of his day are twenty-four.
His body is unsafe at all times, precariously balanced between forces that may at any moment maim or annihilate
it before disease can consume it from the inside. His mind
teeters on the narrow edge of sanity; neither he nor anyone else can be certain whether it has slipped over. And
each separate man has his own private nest of insecurities
to add to those of the species — the job, the status, the love
that are always in danger of slipping away. We like to pic-
ture Achilles and Siegfried varnished with a magic kind of
invulnerability; but we know that each of them met a violent death and that the Norse hero Balder was destroyed by
a mere sprig of mistletoe. If this is the sort of end that
comes to the demigods, what ordinary person can feel himself safe and exempt from fear? The seething insecurity
inside each of us is like a witch's brew, the ingredients of
which are not mentioned in the pharmacopoeia of traditional rationalism.

" Security " is a word of many meanings, certain of which are known to philosophers of law. Some refer to the stability of the political and social order (Aristotle, Polybius, the classical republicans, the American Federalists, Hobbes, and all defenders of despotism whether political or clerical). Others emphasize security in connection with physical safety, property rights, and the fulfillment of contracts (Hume, Bentham, Demogue, Pound). But regarding the inner terrors that come by night, and the anxieties of the working day, they have sadly little to say. Apparently it has been assumed that the reign of law has no concern with the prevalence of fear and guilt, that their respective realms are unrelated and have no common border or exchange of envoys. At any rate, if, as social psychologists have indicated, there is some functional tie between law and the inner security of individual men, it has not been given recognition in legal philosophy.

When we turn to the literature of *general* philosophy, we ought to bear certain meaningful considerations in mind. In the first place, philosophy has almost everywhere shown the effects of an aristocratic bias, and the characteristic pose of the professional philosopher has been one of exemption from the foibles and distractions of common men. Philosophy has traditionally conceived of itself as a rational undertaking and accordingly it has established the custom of disparaging the nonrational or even ignoring it. Moreover, until the latter part of the eighteenth century social change was generally slow enough that philosophers were not compelled to grapple with human insecurity: if people felt insecure it was because they were participants in a defective and rationally remediable pattern, not because they were caught up in a maelstrom of social adjustments.

It must not be forgotten that there have been several eras of human history when security seemed rather irrelevant to the leaders of thought. Security and insecurity express themselves in bodily sets: security as relaxation, insecurity as tension, alertness. One is like a civilian regime, the other like a military. Now, tension or prolonged alertness can lead to exhaustion, to frayed, combative nerves, and imaginary fears. No dog that always has his ears up is a happy dog. We need to let attention lag from time to time, for attention = at tension, and to be aware = to beware. These are the feelings of the age in which we live; we have had too many years of being on guard.

But the early Stoics (especially Cleanthes) made tension their essential principle in physics, psychology, and ethics. Marlowe, Goethe, Ibsen, Theodore Roosevelt, James, and Bergson created in their several ways cults of the strenuous. To them the desire for security was mere flabbiness and rather contemptible. Perhaps they were right, but our time is too weary, too badly shaken.[1]

Leaving aside William James and the rest of these robust

[1] Here is the troubled posture of our time:

"And drawn on by my eager desire, anxious to behold the great abundance of the varied and strange forms created by the artificer Nature, having wandered for some distance among the overhanging rocks, I came to the mouth of a huge cavern before which for a time I remained stupefied, not having been aware of its existence, my back bent to an arch, my left hand clutching my knee, while with the right I made a shade for my lowered and contracted eyebrows; and I was bending continually first one way and then another in order to see whether I could discern anything inside, though this was rendered impossible by the intense darkness within. And after remaining there for a time, suddenly there were awakened within me two emotions, fear and desire, fear of the dark threatening cavern, desire to see whether there might be any marvelous thing therein." [2] The Notebooks of Leonardo Da Vinci 526 (MacCurdy ed. 1945).

mavericks (every one of whom would be suspect at a philosophers' convention), what do we learn about security
from the general tradition of reflective thought?   Not very
much.   Few philosophers have even taken notice that such
a need exists in the human frame.   The closest classic approach was that of Epicurus, who admonished his followers how to become safe from the remainder of humanity
and from the fear of eventual death.   This theme of his has
been repeated with subtle variations and may be considered
philosophy's traditional contribution.   Security is deemed
achieved when one orders his affairs and his inner life in
such a way that the favors and threats of men and gods
are alike indifferent to him.

Of course, Epicurus was right in part; the security he described is a real one and at times not only desirable but attainable.   It may be called *isolative*, since its success depends upon the extent to which one can seal the doors and
windows of his personality and cut off the emotional currents of human intercourse.   If we were to follow Dame
Intellectual Fashion, we would first denigrate, then discard
isolative security; but the sounder course is to suspend
judgment on the subject until deeper voices have been
heard.

The opposite of isolative is *parasitic* security.   In its
more obvious manifestations this involves dependence
upon some charismatic leader, party council, or ecclesiastical body.   One is secure because the leader or the priest is
there — to answer questions, to exorcise doubts, and to
send scapegoats out into the wilderness.   Security is not
something original or inherent, but derivative; not generated but drawn down.   It is easy to regard the parasitic se-

curity of others with an attitude of supercilious contempt,
and many of us feel all the securer in doing so. But if we
look closely at this kind of comfort, we find that since it is
obtained at secondhand it strangely resembles parasitism.
Is it nobler to found one's security on those deemed infe-
rior than on those deemed superior?

Parasitic security has some subtle guises. For example,
it characterizes the attitude of the positivists in sociological
science, including sociological jurisprudence, toward the
whole complex problem of values. There is no need, we
are told, to praise or blame, advocate or condemn, existing
social standards; our discipline confines itself to investigat-
ing a society or culture and endeavoring to ascertain the
values that control its life. This amounts to saying that the
society, like the leader, knows best. Naturally, the positivist finds it much easier to show the burgeoning variety of
values in the different cultures than to assess and reform
those of his own time and place. Perhaps this instance may
suggest to any self-critical reader that parasitic security is
not necessarily or invariably someone else's.

Then there is *participative* security. It partakes of the
isolative in so far as the individual creates and contributes,
of the parasitic in so far as he draws from others. Its dis-
tinguishing trait is an irreducible duality, for in achieving
participative security a man must feel safety simultaneously for and through himself and for and through the
group. The group (for example, the labor union) is safeguarded, but not at the cost of his insecurity. He survives
within the stronghold of the group. Participative security
is no simple elixir; in fact, a particular group may turn out
to be a poison instead of a tonic.

At this point, conventional dialectic practice would require that we establish a deceptively obvious distinction between objective security on the one hand and subjective security on the other. It would say: Is a man safe just because he thinks he is? Is he unsafe just because he fears? To these intendedly rhetorical questions our general answer is an obstinate " Yes." We decline to sever our subject along the lines of such a distinction, precisely because a man may become safe or unsafe in society by thinking himself secure, safe or unsafe by listening to the voice of his own fears. The a priori separation of subjective from objective security unprofitably ignores the power in a human being to procreate either safety or jeopardy for himself. In view of that power, we ought to regard security as pervasive and entire; when its cosmos has to be split, a stronger cleaver than dialectic convenience is called for.

Here, however, we are interested not in cleaving and dividing our subject but in identifying it as best we can. And since the philosophers' neglect of security seems to be due to their aristocratic and rationalistic biases, the logical course for us is to leave them and to turn to other sources which have been free of those particular shortcomings. We pass then from Epicurus to Lucretius; *i.e.*, to the poets who have shared the experience of insecurity and have left us descriptions or at least hints of its nature. Of course, religious poets will offer the most instructive guidance because they are centrally concerned with human insecurity and the sufferings it entails.

But before consulting them a brief reminder is in order. The reader will perhaps remember that, when we were trying to ascertain what " freedom " meant in human experience, we derived a helpful suggestion from genetic psychology. We were told by the psychologists that a very young infant shows reactions of anger when he is held too tightly and his movements are constricted. But, in the same connection, we were also informed that a sudden loss of support will cause the infant to show fear reactions. Here then is a significant clue: insecurity may be genetically related to the *fear of falling*.

Certainly, there is nothing ambiguous about " falling " in the poetic literature of religion. Man's first corruption is described as a " fall," and so was the punishment of Lucifer, son of the morning. Sacred books are full of references to slippings, castings down, and slidings, quicksands and quagmires, holes, chasms, pits, and depths. Sins and lapses from grace are denominated falls, and the destination of the sinner, being underground, accords with the gravitational path of a fall. To be insecure in the symbolism of religious poetry means to be in peril of losing one's footing and falling down. Would these metaphors recur so often or strike so deep if they did not touch what is familiar in individual experience?

Consistently enough, the same sources frequently though not invariably identify security with a firm footing. The virtuous man plants his feet on solid ground; he cannot be moved. Sometimes the solidity of the terrain is such that it is called " a rock " on which either he or his house is said to stand. As insecurity is awareness of the quicksand, the slough, or the pit, so security is the satisfying feel of eternal bedrock. To the individual, then, security means firm and lasting support, insecurity the fear of its loss.

There is no difficulty in translating these concepts of religious poetry into the language of social relations. In that language, the texture of the individual's footing — the ground under his feet — depends upon his having a stake in the goods of his society, on his feeling that he belongs in it and that others accept and approve his belonging. By belonging, he is held upright; he is supported. The whole complex fabric of society exists to keep him from falling. If, however, it should disapprove and reject him, he senses that the support will be withdrawn, leaving him to drop into some bottomless pit. This is the danger that haunts every one of us, most of all those among us who show their uneasiness by strutting and blustering as they go along. This is what we mean by " insecurity " in the province of legal philosophy — it is the fear of loss of social support.

Now, of course, society never was like a rock in firmness or stability. It has always been in a process of change, so that men's footing has at no time matched the hard immovability of the religious ideal. But, where change has been slow and gradual enough, generations could live out their lives before the new forces shook down the accustomed structure and so insecurity was reserved primarily for the oppressed and underprivileged castes. To them the social organization offered little or no foothold. What security they could find was likely to be isolative (*e.g.*, Epictetus) on the one hand, or parasitic (*e.g.*, Messianism) on the other.

Change has speeded up in the past two centuries and accordingly security on all levels, including the most privileged, has been transformed. The social fabric does not feel like a rock any more, even under the soles of our most prosperous fellow citizens. It remains nevertheless a chief support. Education and daily experience admonish us to rely on it as we pass through the experiences of our days, to plant our feet on its surface and grip it as best we can. But we can feel it throb and move beneath us. It feels less like a rock than like a moving platform which not only holds men up but carries them along. The foothold we have now is on a surface in motion and nothing is to be gained by imagining that it will stand still. The motion, needless to say, need not impair our sensation of security. If it is properly adapted, it can imitate the soothing reassurance of the womb and the cradle.[2]

Once we decide to consider the fabric of social relations as a sort of moving platform that either affords security by supplying one with firm footing or creates insecurity by threatening to let one fall, it is no longer difficult to systematize a study of the legal material applicable to the subject. Our moving platform can be so readily assimilated to a ship at sea that its strength and stability will almost inevitably suggest a hull and a keel. And if we follow these obvious indications, we can analyze the law's relations to human security under the headings: The Hull and the Keel; The Rail and the Cabin; The Chart and the Motive Power. These together should clarify the function of law in strengthening or weakening the individual's security; *i.e.*, his sensation of social upholding. Of one thing we can be certain at the very start: the passengers cannot dispense with the ship. " There is no such thing in a civilized society as self-support." [3]

[2] Plato recommended soothing small children by rocking them: "it is like having them always rocked — if that were possible — on the sea." **Laws** 790C–D (Loeb's trans. 1942), II, 11.

[3] Bellamy, Looking Backward 104 (Mod. Lib. ed. 1942).

II. *The Hull and the Keel*

Facing the Judge. In any appraisal of law's contribution to the strength of social support, the first conspicuous criterion will be the quality of the judges. Why do the bones of the most callous cynic turn to water whenever his imagination depicts the ominous silences of a courtroom, the witness stand, the searchings and prying of adversary counsel, and the ultimate solemnity of the judge's decision? It is a place where you can barely hear strange whisperings in some alien incantative tongue. From time to time the lawyers gather to confer up there where judgment sits in its priestly robes. What do they say? Why cannot everyone hear? The layman is told he may not address the court; he may not even volunteer the truth of the case; he may not testify to what he heard said, or what he thought, or why he did what he did. What kind of a place is this where all the ordinary practices of daily life are forbidden and a grown man can be silenced like some helpless child while others dispose of his property, his reputation, or his liberty? It is an awesome thing to go forward before the judge and await the utterance of his decision. The whole of society speaks through him; all its force is marshaled behind his pronouncement. He symbolizes the merger of conceptual justice with organized coercion, the rational humane with the mass brute. To him have been remitted the ideals of his culture and the power to compel submission. When a citizen stands in court he feels the immediate impact of that power; it is all assembled and concentrated there on him. A trial is certainly a hateful ordeal, but there is at least some comfort in the probability that it will reach an outcome of justice provided the judge is honest.

Some judges are not honest. They sell their decisions either for money or for political gain. Judgments may be bought in their chambers, at their homes, or by a mere call on the telephone. And we are told that such men sleep at night, digest their food, and laugh with their companions. Some judges who would refuse bribes of money or political favor make themselves implements of persecution and oppression. To them the law is what the party or the church would have it be; the " facts " are changed to fit the shape of some preconceived result. Such were the judges of Hitler's Germany and of Mussolini's Italy. We have heard of no instance in which a Soviet judge has, by resisting arbitrary executive action, given meaning to Article 112 of his country's constitution (" Judges are independent and subject only to the law."). In the Union of South Africa and in the United States of America there are some judges who read the law through bifocal spectacles, the upper lens being reserved for men of the white race.[4]

The quality of the judges helps to determine the conduct of the police. The policeman is theoretically a guardian of law-abiding citizens, a living instrument of social safety and peace. Why then is he frequently distrusted and feared in the slum areas where he is most needed? Sometimes it is because he knows that the magistrates will tolerate brutality if the victim is poor enough. The law in daily application is thus made to vary from neighborhood to neighborhood. It is understandable that so-called respectable citizens, including legal philosophers, may pass

---

[4] What is in store for such judges can be found in Canto XXI of Dante's Inferno.

through their lives unacquainted with this diversity in the regime of " law."

On the whole, the social support that a legal system can supply depends less on substantive rules or technical refinements than on the daily behavior of the officials. If judges and policemen are upright, they help to hold the citizens upright whatever the wisdom of the positive code. Of course this is not to say that the specific dispositions of law are indifferent; on the contrary, they can go far to influence the attitude and conduct of the officials.

It is a seeming paradox that the law often serves social support best by recognizing its own limitations, by self-contraction. To heighten the paradox, self-contraction may go forward under a conceptual slogan of expansion. The scope of law in such instances is said to grow, but with each expansion the power actually exerted by aid of law may be found to shrink. For example, when the United States Supreme Court held, in the restrictive covenants cases, that action by state courts was the making of " law " under the Fourteenth Amendment, it simultaneously extended the meaning of law and contracted the authority of law's organs.[5] When it recognized that a labor union (an

[5] The cases arose out of the widespread practice of inserting in deeds and other documents relating to real property a provision that the property could not be sold to members of some designated racial group or groups. State courts had generally enforced these " restrictive covenants," and had thus abetted the harmful purposes which they were designed to serve. The Fourteenth Amendment to the Constitution provides that no state shall " deny to any person within its jurisdiction the equal protection of the Laws." This amendment controls state action only; it does not prohibit individual acts of discrimination. The Supreme Court at long last held that, though individuals might be free to enter into these invidious covenants, the action of a state court in *enforcing* such an agreement would be *state* action which denied equal protection of the laws. In short, the discriminatory covenants could not be enforced by means of the law. Shelley v. Kraemer, 334 U. S. 1 (1948).

extragovernmental order) had been vested with certain governmental authorities, it required the union to desist from racial discrimination; that is, *pro tanto* to conduct itself like an arm of government.[6] One of the ways of the law is to merge other orders into its own and thus to limit them. It gives them narrower channels along with their new force. This continuing process can impose greater and greater social responsibility on all orders brought within the orbit of law. What was formerly spontaneous and more or less irresponsible assumes responsibility and the discipline of system.

This movement should encourage the individual citizen to feel that progressively more available force is subordinated to his physical and psychic security, that his neighbors will be both comforted and restrained by the same conviction, and that the several orders under law and law itself will act from day to day to build his safety.[7] To these assurances honest judges are indispensable. They are indispensable because injustice either suffered or witnessed is empathically identified by the human organism as a species of attack. Man's sense of injustice, with its miracle of imaginative interchange, recognizes the approach of danger and summons his glandular, nervous, and muscular resources to the defense. And how much more hotly an out-

[6] Steele v. Louisville & N. R. R., summarized on p. 29, note 20.

[7] A revolutionary does not like a society containing too many revolutionaries: he needs some continuity and order while he changes the old structure. A robber would not like a lawless society: he needs law-abiding citizens to accumulate goods for him; if the police become too lax, he will have more competitors than prospective victims. Robin Hood could not have enjoyed the Greenwood had there been no Sheriff of Nottingham. So it is that even those who break the law in some particular category expect its enforcement in all others.

rage will be felt where the attack is seen to be perpetrated by a judge, whose precise office it is to repel such injuries. A judgment ruled by the judge's party interest of the moment is an immediate assault on all outside the party and a threat to the eventual safety of those within. A judgment ruled by bribes is a deadly affront to everyone; like the Praetorian Guard in the decadent days of the Roman Empire, it auctions the sovereignty of society to the highest bidder. Unless the courts deserve confidence, no one is safe.

The Use of Bulkheads. Marine architects have long since learned the advantages of bulkheads. If successive watertight compartments are installed in the hold of a vessel, though one may be flooded, the others will furnish buoyancy. Thus there may be temporary injury without final disaster. The ship is securer in the multiplicity of its supports.

The state and society too are equipped with bulkheads which law may be seen to supply or safeguard. If law fails to supply them, the individual citizen will endeavor to build his own. Some of them, as we shall see, he simply must fashion for himself, some will be fashioned for him by social groups; but it is calamitous to leave him any major portion of the whole task. For then fear, unless it acts to emasculate his spirit entirely, will drive him to an unending series of mad precautions. Trembling and obsessed with the phantasm of an isolative security, he will construct one futile chamber after another until he evokes the very dangers he had thought to avoid. There can never be enough of privately provided bulkheads in an unseaworthy society. And manifestly, if a society fails to afford sustenance for such periods as old age, illness, the years of schooling, the bearing and nurturing of children, and unemployment, that society is not wholly seaworthy. These then are bulkheads which it is the law's function to build.

To make certain that there are multiple supports in the social structure, law must sometimes be used to safeguard the walls between its own chambers and those outside its scope. That is, law may be used to preserve the assurance that the citizen does not depend upon it alone. It may enforce the separation of church and state, the autonomy of social groupings, the independence of private educational institutions, the freedom of the press, and the privacy of personal, marital, and familial relations. To keep these bulkheads intact, the legal system can alternatively insist that they are not within its province at all or that, though within its province, they are exempt by constitutional provision or public policy from its regulative machinery. Only a jurist who has unlimited confidence in his own wisdom will be willing to impair these extrajuridical bulkheads and even he may be given pause when he considers his brothers and successors on the bench.

The law has good reason to know the advantages of self-restraint. Its own bulkheads have been divided and subdivided down the course of its history, until now the idea of restricted risk or limited liability may be called its central principle. And here it shows a progressive adaptation to human needs, for except in case of impending shipwreck, desperate love, or similar calamity man desires in all things to hedge his commitments. The development of law may be profitably viewed as a manifold effort to limit liability.

We have moved a long distance since the days when a complainant under the Roman procedure had to agree in advance that, if the accused should be acquitted, he, the initiator of the prosecution, would bear an equal penalty, or since Icelandic litigants of the Njals Saga [8] invited outlawry or banishment by submitting their controversies to adjudication. The law has slowly learned to limit the stakes that parties must risk. The machinery may take a man's coat but not strip him, strip him naked but send him out free, imprison him but not kill him, hang him by the neck but not taint the blood of his children.[9] The rules for pleading and for the framing of issues are techniques to limit liability. The business corporation, the availability of divorce, the right to resign from public office or private trust, and the discharge from bankruptcy are such techniques. So too are the rules governing geographic jurisdiction for the service of process, the scope of examinations, the admissibility of evidence, the procedures for appellate review, and the purging of contempts. Taxation is of course a technique for restricting the citizen's otherwise unlimited liability to furnish services to his government. Every statutory or constitutional confinement of official action fulfills the same purpose. In short, although

[8] This Icelandic saga of the twelfth or thirteenth century presents one of the most graphic descriptions of primitive litigation and thus helps to explain many peculiar attributes of contemporary Anglo-Saxon practice. Kocourek and Wigmore, Evolution of Law Series, Sources of Ancient and Primitive Law, c. VI (1915).

[9] As the history of the common law goes, it is not so long since the exclusively Kentish custom of permitting a felon's son to inherit his farm was considered odd enough to inspire "The father to the bough, the son to the plough." St. Germain, Doctor and Student I, x (1518). It was not until 1814 that the British Parliament began gradually to abolish "corruption of the blood." 54 Geo. III, c. 145. Meanwhile the American abhorrence of this senseless penalty had been expressed in Art. III, Sec. 3, of the Constitution.

we do not always know in advance just how great a given risk may be, we can be assured that under the law it has certain rationally intelligible limits.

The Incidence of Change. The concept of limitation of liability is one of the intrinsic principles with which law can serve to humanize social change. Change, of course, there must be — continual, radical, perpetually disturbing, and, so far as we can judge, at least temporarily accelerating. Change automatically entails consequences of anxiety and suffering; it is wholly welcome only to those who have nothing to lose. Since new adjustments are inevitable throughout social, technological, and economic relations, the pragmatic objective is not resistance but manipulation, not submission but intelligent alleviation. To recognize the inexorability of change need not instill insecurity, provided that the canon of limited liability is known to be respected.

Limited liability in the province of social change implies four basic criteria. These are: (1) that social change will be kept within certain limits of pace; (2) that social change will be effected by use of certain methods; (3) that social change will be kept within certain wide limits of substance; and, most important of all, (4) that the gains and losses of social change will be felt solidarily; that is, by the whole citizenry in shares. Functionally related each to the others, these criteria can operate to rationalize and reform the incidence of change.

Of course, law offers no panacea for the ills that come with growth or decay in society. Nevertheless, as experience shows, it can at least modify the pace of new forces and can cushion their collisions with human lives. Who will doubt that, if a proclamation emancipating Negro slaves had been issued during the American Revolutionary War, the course of economic and social as well as legal history would have been altered? Who will deny that the enactment of civilian rather than military control of atomic energy has deflected the destiny of this generation? The instrument's value resides in the wisdom of those who use it.

To talk of the pace of social change would be rather meaningless unless we apply some standard of reference. In a study of change and insecurity, there appears only one decisive standard, and that is the human psychosomatic constitution. What in short does pace of change signify to men?

Clearly, nothing is more necessary to the health of the human organism than an adequate allowance of continuity in psychic experience. Discontinuity in small doses evokes surprise accompanied sometimes by resentment, sometimes by laughter; discontinuity in larger doses evokes fear and insecurity. The acme of discontinuity is madness. There is in us a sort of co-ordinative set, a subconscious leaning on continuation that must not be betrayed too abruptly or too often. If you change all the furniture in your room, item by item and slowly enough, it remains the same room; fast enough, it becomes a different room, still yours; fast and often enough, it loses its identity as your room and its use as your orientation. Of course, over sufficient time all our cultural furniture is fated to be changed. We too shall eventually become subjects for modern history, then medieval, then ancient, even for the archaeologist. But the human life span and capacity for adjustment must delimit the pace; men do not willingly regard themselves as primitives.

There is indeed a biological value in continuity. Revolutionaries perceiving this sooner or later wrap themselves in the ripped integuments of the *ancien régime*. But the continuity is one of movement. It is never discrete or stagnant, never conducive to smugness or complacency. Granted that human adaptability to change has certain limits, the accelerations of the past century indicate that those limits can be pushed outward, that custom can habituate men to the sudden emergence of new conditions. And where change has effected the highest measure of discontinuity (*e.g.*, the Christian Revolution, the French Revolution, the American Civil War, the Soviet Revolution), it has been preceded by such a lag in the rational application of available legal reforms that existence had already lost continuity for a major segment of the people. Some modicum of gratifying expectation is indispensable to us because the scintilla of the passing present, which is all we ever have, is so largely compounded of what we hope to be.

One of law's advantages as governor of the pace of change is its own characteristic and notorious continuity. The legal system stands as a symbol of persistence, retaining familiar habiliments while it undertakes new duties. Its language is old, its costumes archaic, and there is something of comfort even in its ceremonial and redundancy. Here at least is a known landmark. Here is an institution where antique machinery may be repaired but is never quite wholly replaced, where procrastination can continue to mock the frenzied impatience outside. Law musters up the proud, nostalgic associations of the past. Through every vicissitude it endures somehow with its ancient precedents and established rules. For even when a judge invents his own law and concocts his version of the facts, he will not fail to profess obedience to the accepted tradition.

Then, again, what is any system of property law if not an assurance that certain relations among men will move along predetermined, unbroken paths? The house that others must respect as mine today they must equally respect tomorrow; the promise I receive today I can trust tomorrow. If there is to be a change in these relations, it too must emanate from sources within the known categories of the law. The legal system quietly informs men that their spontaneous and accidental groupings may become firm and formal associations, that their casual promises may be traded for dependable expectations, and that social arrangements endowed with more than passing expediency may rise to the dignity of institutions. Whatever the tenure apparatus — private, co-operative, socialized, or mixed — it affords law's projection of momentary attitudes into future purposes. It receives and carries over, and is thus a technique of psychic transition. And even the changes and permutations within the law will bear the stamp of the familiar tradition.

The received tradition may have magic of its own. There is a special courage that comes, for instance, from the knowledge that one's legal order contains the fruits of ancestral struggles for liberty. This knowledge can counsel individuals to be brave in social pioneering because others were brave before them; it can admonish them to abstain from oppression because earlier oppressors had to sign a Magna Charta or had to ride in tumbrels. Such admonitions, drawn perhaps from popular misreading of history, become part of a national epos, part of the political and economic mores.

For example, to the enlightened American of our time "equal but *separate*" facilities for Negroes in transportation, housing, or education is a repulsive formula and he criticizes the Supreme Court for tolerating it. He will in all likelihood forget that in its original purport, reflecting the social influences of an earlier day, the phrase would more accurately read "separate but *equal*." His very oversight shows how far Negro rights have advanced in the interval and how greatly the legal machinery (*e.g.*, fair employment practice commissions, hampered though they have been) can contribute to the pace of that movement. Thus the law creates new expectations as it fills or disappoints the old; and when these arise from invidious distinctions of race or religion the vocation of law is not patience but cogence.

The legal system is that institution to which men look first when their daily sustenance is imperiled. One of the expectations of citizens in a normal society is that the law will appropriately safeguard their opportunities for employment and advancement and their co-equal right to participate in the goods of their time and place. In the twentieth century a legal order that does not endeavor to meet this expectation is usually replaced by one that does, and the latter generally resorts to state ownership of some major part of the means of production. The resultant change in the tenure system need inflict no more suffering than the English Statute de Donis [10] or the Virginia act abolishing fees tail, unless it is violently resisted, violently executed, or installed without payment of compensation to expropriated owners.   Hatred of the latter has often blinded the new regime to the practical advantages of paying compensation.   Too often governments, by withholding the award in money, have conferred a crown of martyrdom on otherwise contemptible groups.   They have forgotten that money is the cheapest of all mediums of payment.

Let us suppose that during a time of war scientists at work in laboratories provided for them by the military discover some new and stupendously effectual source of industrial power.   The discovery if put to civilian uses could be expected to supersede immense existing investments in patents, plants, machinery, and transmission lines.   What a fearful dilemma!   The threatened impact on the lives of the citizens perplexes imagination and makes the men of government quail under the burden of their responsibility. If permission to employ the new power should be granted incontinently, it would strike like a whirlwind the millions of small entrepreneurs, employees, and persons dependent on modest holdings of the affected investments.   If, on the other hand, the action should be retarded in order to protect certain obsolescent industries (enabling the men in control meanwhile to sell their holdings to the gullible), the public would bear an unconscionable loss.   Such a nation could be said to have a revolution in its womb, prom-

[10] This statute (13 Edw. I, c. I) was enacted in 1285 under pressure of the great landowners.   It greatly extended, if it did not initiate, the entailing of estates and thus severely restricted the right of owners to alienate their real property.

ising shorter hours of work, cheaper goods, abundance, and leisure, and threatening mass unemployment, panic, and bankruptcy. The method of delivery would prove as decisive as the discovery itself. Possibly, the laws would give over the invention to large corporate formations and thus subvert it to the uses of irresponsible monopoly and private gain. Moreover, the laws might, by failing to regulate and graduate its application, leave it free to shatter the walls and pillars of the society. Finally, there is the possibility that statutes might be enacted adequate in enlightenment to the power they dispose and designed to benefit the future without making a nightmare of the present. In effect, these several decisions would shape a new social constitution, and for ultimate blessing or curse the decisions would be taken under the procedures of law. Being congenitally unable to abandon their anticipative posture, the men of such an era would elect to assume that there were somewhere resources of wisdom equal to the occasion. And indeed the very crassness of that assumption might call them forth.

The Arcs of Oscillation. Given our present velocity of social change, the support under foot feels dangerously unstable. *Everyman* walks with the figment of a skull in his hand, and the skull is his own. The unemployed, the dispossessed, and the undernourished constantly remind him that tomorrow may be wholly unlike today, that the complex fabric of economic relations may be torn at any moment, and that he may become superfluous to his society. Even in slower eras of transformation men have anxiously scanned the developments of their time to learn what was portended for themselves as passive particulars in the universal flux. When, for example, a certain sublime religious tragedy took place and the veil of the Temple (we are told) was rent, some poor weaver must have clapped his hands and rejoiced over the prospect of mending it. And when Columbus returned to report his adventures, some Venetian merchant hearing them must have tossed and fretted in an uneasy sleep. Nowadays it is hardly to be doubted that workmen, as they manufacture industrial conveyor belts, wonder whose jobs are being displaced and how long their own can last.

The law deals with two major types of social change; that is, the changes resulting from new inventions, discoveries, technological advances, and other modifications of the factual substratum, and changes resulting from the acts of men under law's own authority. The honest observer in this generation must concede that there are scarcely any tenable limits to either type. We are no more able than the wisest of our predecessors to predict the shape of the future society or to assume that it will retain any specific outline. The legal system can encourage or deter inventors but cannot make their inventions for them; it can dissolve or protect spontaneous social groupings but cannot by its own fiat call them into being. Are there then any bounds which law should set, so that though the support may rock it will not buckle and collapse? Assuming that law has rationally endeavored to regulate the tempo of social oscillation, can we say that there is an arc beyond which lies disaster?

The angle of that extreme arc is delimited by the point on its path where two lines of human equality simultaneously intersect it. This is the point at which passive and active equality can be seen to converge in the given circumstances. Equality is a claim primitive enough to set bounds to social change though no other interest could. The demand for equality arises as soon as the human infant can recognize any duality in which he himself is a component integer; and, since man is a congenitally classificatory animal, that experience begins very early and continues within one group or another throughout the span of life. To perceive someone else's resemblance in any relevant respect is to clamor for equal treatment. It is a perception so congenial to humanity that we have to be educated to the missing of it.

Passive equality as a limitation of social change has to do with the residual status of those individuals who suffer the impact of the transformation. It postulates that whatever they lose they must somehow retain the attributes of equal members of their society. If they are stripped of property, for instance, they must sink no lower than others who previously had no property, and must continue to exhibit the traits and enjoy the rights of citizenship. If it is employment that they lose in some technological metamorphosis, that deprivation must not prejudice their equal claim to the concern of their government. They must be able to discern limits to their fears. For particularly where the laws are the active agency of social change, failure to ensure passive equality will leave all citizens anxious and insecure.

What are the minimal human attributes that the law should assure? To this kind of question the sense of injustice offers only an *ad hoc* answer. It can assert with firm confidence that the treatment of the dispossessed peasantry who became urban workers during the Industrial

Revolution, the treatment of the American Indians by the United States (including its judiciary), the treatment of the kulaks in the Soviet collectivization of agriculture — all of these violated passive equality. In each case the sufferers from social change were allowed or forced to sink below the level of citizenship as defined in their own polity. And we should add the harrowing example of the " Okies " whom California endeavored to stamp as pariahs and exclude from its borders. In a despotic society — to take the darkest kind of setting — all the citizens may be dispossessed of elementary civil rights and thus all will be passively equal; but even under such a government a reform that callously imposes imprisonment or execution on expropriated groups is no genuine leveling but a summons to suspicion and conspiracy.

Under the Roman law a *socius* (one who joined his labor or capital with another's in some common holding or enterprise) could by agreement be wholly excluded from sharing in the losses of the *societas* but he could not be excluded from all participation in its profits. This rule illustrates the meaning of active equality in the incidence of social change. All members of a society, including particularly those who bear the losses consequent on a given transformation, should receive shares in its benefits and advantages. Some may be exempted at least temporarily from the sufferings, but none should be barred from the enjoyments, if law is to convey a sense of support in the flux.

Active equality is the particular claim of those injured by social advance. Let us take the example of American workers about to be displaced by a system of conveyor belts. They see an unemployment insurance law which determines their employer's contribution to the general fund by the size not of his sales but of his pay roll. In short, by discharging them, he will create unemployment and by that very act reduce his pay-roll tax. As his costs go down his profits rise; but the displaced workers and all others in their plight will receive decreasing means of assistance from him and the industry to which he belongs. Thus they are barred from participation in the fruits of this technological advance. At that, they will probably fare better than the forgotten Indian " wards," doomed by law to sit and contemplate the widening gap between their disseisors and themselves. They know they have no solidary stake in the national society. And as long as such exclusion is visibly possible under a dispensation of democratic law, everyone has cause to examine his position and to fear.

We have been testing the hull and the keel of social support. They have given no clear demonstration of strength or stability in tempestuous seas. At this point, we report only that there can be no strength *unless* judges exhibit integrity, unless liabilities have limits assigned to them, and unless the laws reserve for human life some modicum of continuity; and that there can be no stability *unless* the virile demands of passive and active equality are taken seriously into account in the framing of major policies. Facing these propositions helps to elucidate the extent of contemporary man's predicament and the causes of his anxiety. Yet there have also appeared some few sanctions for hope or at least for resolve, which encourage us to investigate further.

III. *The Cabin and the Rail*

The Value of Seclusion. As a general rule the regime of law stops at the door of a citizen's cabin and contents itself with protecting his right to shut out intruders. The cabin was traditionally a house sufficiently detached from the dwellings of neighbors to insulate its occupants and their doings. But it need not be a house; now it is likely to be an apartment or a hotel room. In an authentic sense, we all — like tortoises — carry our cabins with us wherever we go, and this too is something of which the philosophy of law should take account.

Some sort of cabin is indispensable. A place must be provided where the regulative pressures of society are relaxed and an individual can resume his native stature. In the cabin he is away from the haughty stare, the frown, the putting forth of the finger, and the oppressive policings of social order. He can open his collar there and can give vent to his own particular daydreams, his mutterings and snatches of crazy song, his bursts of obscenity and afflatus of glory. If he does not disturb the neighbors, he can either fondle his woman or beat her. The outside and its laws would be intolerable were it not for four walls that may close them off. Social discipline, whether legal or extralegal, needs the cabin to safeguard its own effectuality; in short, it needs a place where men can feel safe from it.

The law, however, has always exerted some influence on thought and action within the home, if only because it determines the structural patterns of sexual and familial relations. The statutes of a given state may, by prohibiting divorce or by exaggerating parental authority, convert the cabin into a trap, so that the conformities required outside seem light and easy compared to those exacted within. Outside at least there remains always some small area for self-assertion, some residual anonymity. Finally, even when law most fully respects the seclusions of the cabin, it nevertheless stands like a customs inspector regulating what can pass in and what can come forth; and this is law's most cogent means of determining the content of interior life. For instance, the beginning of an evolution in family structure and relations may incubate with considerable irresponsibility inside the walls; but once it ventures out-of-doors into the social environs it will be confronted with the disciplines and resistances established by law. These in turn react upon the progress of adjustments within the home and upon the manifold anxieties experienced there.

Of the kinds of anxiety that may be discerned inside a cabin, one of the deepest and most persistent is the experience of guilt. That experience presents an area of concomitance between the causes of human insecurity which are undifferentiate and ubiquitous, and those causes which are specifically identified with the operations of law. Because of this concomitance, guilt is as familiar to ethics and to individual and social psychology as it is to legal theory. There is therefore good reason to expect that even a limited examination of the interplay between law and guilt anxieties would furnish us with considerable light.

Concerning Legal Guilts. Now, if only because the *general* desert of any human being is so difficult of ad-measurement, civilized law properly concerns itself with *particular* desert, which for our present purposes can be narrowed down to particular guilt. When Edmund Burke spoke to advocate Anglo-American conciliation, he insisted there was no way of drawing an indictment against a whole people, charging it with any single kind of guilt; conversely, there is no rational way to draw an indictment against a single individual charging him with general guiltiness. No one person has succeeded in exhausting the entire calendar of crimes, and no mature legal procedure has the facilities to establish so monstrous a vice. Like the Ten Commandments, the law formulates its list of offenses, charges an accused on one or more counts of particular guilt, and makes its adjudication accordingly. But what if its own administration should instill the general guilt with which it professes to be unconcerned?

We will understand the problem readily if we begin with the familiar example afforded by penological experience. Suppose a bank teller is convicted of embezzlement; *i.e.*, a guilt particular as to kind, date, and circumstances of temptation. If after his term of imprisonment his society rejects him as a branded felon, he approaches a state of general guilt, an imputation of pervasive viciousness. Thus cast out he will probably conduct himself as one conscious of general guilt might be expected to. He will develop an obsessive fear of police and courts and a hatred of the social order which so smugly despises him. He feels sure that if arrested again he will be found guilty, whatever the nature of the charge. He regards himself as infected and corrupt.

Qualitatively speaking, this predicament is utterly and tragically miserable. It has, however, its quantitative limits because relatively few of us become involved in crimes of the more important types. These crimes have been rather closely defined and we are generally able to discern the various lines that must not be crossed. We know where to halt.

But suppose the old lines were partially erased and some unconnected segments of new lines were sketched here and there? Suppose further that, instead of using certain kinds of prohibited deeds as tests of guilt, the police and the courts choose to prosecute thoughts in the mind, spoken words, casual associations, imputed sympathies and impulses? Then who could ever be confident that sometime, somewhere, somehow he did not commit some species of crime? Each of us would probably be guilty in one particular or another; and since we could never certainly know the limits of our particular guilts — it may have been some indiscreet phrase or equivocal intonation — we must all experience the state of general guilt.

The attitudes resulting from general guilt, interestingly enough, are precisely those that made law primordially necessary to the evolution of organized society. They are the attitudes of suspicion, fear, and hatred, epitomized in *homo homini lupus*. In a primitive culture (the Melanesian Dobus [11]) which, according to anthropologists, lacks the usual forms of elementary legality, every man's hand is raised in malediction or violence against every other man. The Dobus exemplify what it means to live without the right of recourse to law; and in time of stress the twentieth-century despotic police state exemplifies what it means to live under a legal imputation of general guilt. The two conditions are strikingly similar. Each possesses an extraordinary capacity to corrode and sever spontaneous so-

[11] Benedict, Patterns of Culture, c. V (1934).

cial bonds, to turn friends into enemies and confidants into informers.

In any developed society it has probably been easy to find guilt-ridden individuals of humble rank who are prepared to beat their breasts and accuse themselves of the most horrendous crimes.   But unless the prevailing legal administration has instilled a pervasive state of fear and an acceptance of general guilt, leaders and ministers of government, though fallen from favor, are rarely observed in such a penitential pose.   Scenes of self-accusation enacted by apparently stanch personalities appear to be reserved for autocratic police states.

In the Anglo-Saxon countries the problem of self-incrimination bears an entirely different aspect.   The accused's privilege not to testify against himself is confined to withholding such circumstances only as, in the unfolding of legal history, have been constituent elements of some denominated crime.   The privilege is held therefore not to apply to other circumstances (*e.g.*, unpopular political convictions) which, although not within that category under traditional taxonomy, may and often do involve equally grievous penalties.   The application of severe penalties (such as the stigmatizing loss of employment in the civil service) justifies comparable expansion of the privilege against self-incrimination.[12]   In sum, the good society is at very least one in which men can converse before looking around them.

[12] The problem may be considered in terms of the principles governing "penal actions" (proceedings that appear to be civil in character but that involve very grave sanctions).   *See* Hall, General Principles of Criminal Law 212 (1947).   In denaturalization cases, the thinking of certain justices of the Supreme Court has tended in this direction.   Klapprott v. United States, 335 U. S. 601 (1949).

Law and the Burden of Guilt. In the traditions of orthodox religion, guilt (responsibility for sin) has stood forth persistently and prominently. Theological guilt has often been understood as belonging to the entire human species. A man is said to be guilty because he is a man. His guilt is pervasive and undifferentiated; it is believed to corrupt him through and through. Nor has orthodox religion the monopoly of this theme. To the Neoplatonists of every philosophic era, man is corrupt because he is existential, because he has mixed matter, time, and place with his idea. And these kinds of guilt, *i.e.*, the self-accusations that follow from congenital ability to conceive ideals and congenital inability to live them out, are felt to permeate men in all their faculties. The Old Man of the Mountain of Guilt rides the entire human being.

The same emphasis on permeation and saturation can be found in the psychological analysis of guilts and their consequences. A guilt, we are told, may be particular in the incurring or in the external imposition; its effects in terms of psychic and somatic disturbances will be nonetheless general. One who feels guilty may suffer in members that took no part in the act of wrong: the whole self becomes involved. And — to complete the parallel to the concept of sin — whenever the standards of the relevant social group are shifting and imprecise, the risk of incurring guilt can lead to a nightmare of futile precautions.[13] The relentless need to avoid guilt then becomes, in terms of actions and consequences, indistinguishable from guilt itself.

The legal system affects these experiences in various

---

[13] I think it is Leo Tolstoy who tells the story of the man who thought he was made of glass. He took all sorts of ludicrous precautions but nevertheless slipped one day and fell. He exclaimed "Smash!" and died.

ways. In the first place, the law patently creates certain guilts where otherwise none would be perceived. Moreover, if the administration of law imposes what we have called a general guilt, it deepens and exacerbates the wounds that are inflicted in self-accusation. Even an enlightened jural system, such as confines guilts to the identifiable and particular, will in the interest of deterrence from undesirable patterns of conduct instill certain otherwise nonexistent feelings of guilt. These we know may possibly be raised to the level of honorable shame, where their operation need not be accompanied by fear or insecurity.

What law has most to offer to the sufferer from guilt is the inference conveyed by its own existence. Rules of law are themselves social segregations of guilt. These, they tell us, are the particular norms your society insists upon to such a degree that its organized strength will be used to enforce them. If you violate these norms, you need not speculate concerning your guilt; if you do not violate them, you need not speculate concerning your innocence. Of course, as Oscar Wilde rightly reminds us in the " Ballad of Reading Gaol," there are guilts beyond the proscriptions of law. Moreover, there are sanctions beyond its sanctions, for example, commercial or social ostracism. But the law not only retains the most formal and redoubtable threats; in contemporary societies it also tends to restrain or to absorb various threats emanating from other orders, especially where they may appear to rival its own efficacy. Commercial ostracism (boycott) may be prohibited by law, and certain forms of social ostracism (*e.g.*, the restrictive covenant in real property deeds) may be denied enforcement in the courts and thus become less fearsome.

The sole sanctions that are permanently safe from legal interference are the supernatural.

Obviously, only the most insensitive (Holmes's "bad man," for example) will respond so to the therapy of this counsel emanating from the law as never to suffer from a nonjuridical guilt. But the counsel does have substantial value because legal rules embody certain extensive areas of the general morality. Sometimes, as in the very matter of restrictive real-estate covenants, the law actually surpasses the quality of popular practice.

There is another attribute of mature law that may lighten the load of the guilty. This is the principle of expiability. Most modern legal systems regard all offenses as expiable — at a price. The price is usually in money for breaches of contract and suchlike lesser wrongs, time in jail for serious offenses, death for those deemed most heinous. Once the price has been paid, civilized law is generally satisfied [14] and will afford no support to subsequent social persecution of the offender or his family. Granted that the penalty imposed on a recidivist may be increased in the light of his prior convictions, the new penalty remains nevertheless the price of his new crime (those who buy too often can expect the price to rise). But on completion of each payment, the charge will be eradicated for juridical purposes at least. By this means the legal system affords a procedure of expiation and a more or less adequate opportunity for fresh beginnings. The practice of specified penances in institutionalized religion is a tribute to the same principle, for hardly anyone really believes in an absolution without a penance.

[14] The case of Willie Francis, which we considered on page 113, is fortunately an exception.

Then, again, law reduces guilt by supplying the individual with a scapegoat. We are already familiar with this facility in its unattractive applications. We know, for instance, that many an unfortunate (whether or not technically guilty) has been sentenced in order to divert blame from his society or its political administrators. The unemployed worker is jailed for stealing bread, not the minister of state for failing to provide employment. But, in addition to this type of application, the scapegoat principle of law has a different and commendable utility.

The legal order itself serves as a species of scapegoat for all of us. There are occasions when we know that some irredeemable criminal must be put away or done away with. Who will be willing to lock the cell or throw the lethal switch? Not you or I, not the judge who uttered the sentence. In fact, not even the jailer or the executioner — except as mere vicar and instrument of the law. It is the law that confines this Everyman to his cell, the law that burns out his life. And so, by what seems strangely like a parasitic security, we are enabled to sleep in comfort.

Scapegoat law has a broad back. It is able to bear responsibility for the stupidities and insensibilities of legislators and judges, for the gross inequities of economic distribution, and for the failure of the social sciences to maintain pace with physical science and technology. The law is a conceptual order and as such is safe from the electorate, from history, and from the reproaches of professional conscience. For the same reasons, the secret ballot is one of man's cleverest domestic animals: once it is unleashed, it carries all our individual political sins out into the wilderness of majority infallibility.

The Cabin as Personality. The cabin, as we have begun

to see, may be taken as standing for man's peculiar personality, his inner and private self. When we come to think of it in these terms, we face one of the bitterest dilemmas in legal philosophy. It is the dilemma of human identity. On the one hand, every man is a member of the human species and therefore law is suitable to him. On the other hand, every man is himself, *i.e.*, an utterly unique creature, and therefore law is unsuitable to him. Law indeed boasts that it takes no respect of persons, but to one who wishes to live his uniqueness and to escape the facelessness of conceptual man this is precisely what is wrong with law.

In philosophic literature the proposition that law does not respect persons has had two fruitful applications. The first of these is the egalitarian thesis that no one shall be above the law, no one exempt from accountability under its standards. The laws are the ultimate rulers, said Plato and Aristotle, and Coke endeavored to explain the same principle to James I. This thesis has had a variety of functions, historic and contemporary. Its boldest version — even bolder than Coke's — was put into the mouth of Job. When Job's friends (bearing his afflictions and his boils with admirable cheerfulness) insisted that God could not be called to account for the sufferings of the righteous, he expostulated: " Will ye accept his person? will ye contend for God? . . . . He will surely reprove you, if ye do secretly accept persons." [15]

---

[15] Job XIII.8, 10 (King James version). To "accept persons" is a sufficiently accurate translation of the original, which means literally to "lift the face," *i.e.*, to show favor. The overtones of meaning can rarely be preserved in their entirety, however such key terms may be rendered. For example, *Ts'doko*, generally translated "righteousness," is at times closer to the connotations of "justice." I have employed the latter in the quotation at note 24 *infra*.

The second application of " no respect of persons " was also perceived by classical theorists. Their specific concern was to describe the ideal technique for ruling a state. In this connection the laws, Plato said, operate " like an obstinate and ignorant tyrant " [16] because they impose inflexible rules without allowing for changed circumstances or unforeseen exceptional cases. If a supremely wise ruler were to be available, he could do as the pilot, the shepherd, and the physician do: he could direct matters according to the skill of his craft — with or without laws, perhaps better without them. But, no such scientific statesman being at hand in this era, one must turn to the laws and use them to educate and refine as well as to govern the citizens. In fact, Plato submits, good general laws are a necessary attribute of the best kind of state a legislator can reasonably expect to establish. And all subsequent history has endorsed these insights; we can dispense neither with standards nor with wise magistrates to vivify them in particular cases.

Our present dilemma, however, is somewhat different. We are not concerned with the ruler's but with the subject's difficulty. General laws may prove efficient for the purposes of government but bitterly unsuitable to an individual who is not shaped to the anticipated pattern; in short, who is not what his society considers " a reasonable man." He does not quite conform, he is simply himself, and cannot stretch or will not shrink to the prescribed juridical stature. Perhaps he is too gullible to be protected by the laws governing advertisements or too slowly coordinated for the laws governing due care and negligence. Perhaps he really believes his religious creed and goes about

[16] Politicus 294.

denouncing sinners in the most inconvenient (*i.e.*, the highest) places. Perhaps he is some congenital homosexual to whom law means only an ugly mechanism by which he can be intimidated, blackmailed, and sadistically abused.

In the first place, it should be remembered that in modern societies most human needs — even of nonconformists — are mediated through and by means of social groups. This mediation reduces the severity of the problem, for qua participant in a formalized social group the nonconformist is merely another fungible member in contemplation of the statutes applicable to that group. For example, though he converses every day with the shade of Virgil, his labor union will nevertheless bargain on his behalf and establish the terms and conditions of his work.

Fortunately, moreover, the dilemma of the aberrant or " unreasonable " man is not so cruel in the operations of law as popular theory would indicate. Of course, law should not respect persons, particularly the persons of the mighty. Job's outburst was probably the most fragrant incense ever to ascend from an altar. The standards of law provide our best pragmatic technique by which arrogant administrators and executives can be called to book. And when, on the other hand, legal rules are to be applied to the lowly, there is at least a modicum of discretion available to magistrates, juries, policemen, commissioners, and state's attorneys. General rules need not decide deviant particular cases, unless officials are dogmatic, stupid, corrupt, or inhumane. For, to the sense of injustice, an individual's peculiar qualities may be empathized as a constituent part of his predicament and thus they may influence the determination of his desert. We cannot abandon the law's conceptual man without jeopardizing many of the freedoms that the past has won. But the conceptual man is never quite the one in the prisoner's dock. The latter is as God and society have made him, with such alterations as he himself has been able to furnish. The composite impression conveyed by all the circumstances can sway the judge and the jury when they come to their final appreciation of his case. Then it is that a rule of law and a list of facts must be chosen conformably to the general denouement which is felt to be just. So as long as the sense of injustice proffers its imaginative interchange, law may be conformed in its individual applications to many if not all the special needs of nonconformists.

The Intrusive Middle. Too frequently, eminent philosophers have failed to appreciate the dimensions of nonconformance. Being sensitive spirits for the most part, they take care to remain on the lee side of the law, turning meanwhile to an isolative security for their own satisfactions. Most of the lawlessness that they may come to know is confined to the cabin of academic lectures and writings or to the even closer quarters of their private reflections. It is therefore easy for them to assume that laws are quite literally enforced in the outside society; and, being trained by temperament and vocation to take verbal imperatives very seriously, they naïvely believe that sovereign power almost always has its way. That probably is why such gifted thinkers as Locke, Kant, Gény, and Duguit regarded revolution as the sole and unique answer to unjust laws.

But the facts are otherwise, as philosophers might learn by considering the very first sovereign imperative ever addressed to man. That imperative read like this: " Of the tree of the knowledge of good and evil, thou shalt not eat of it; for in the day that thou eatest thereof thou shalt surely die." Now, everyone knows that although Adam ate of the forbidden fruit he did not die in that day but lived to begin the work of husbandry and to suffer certain tragic pains as a parent. Whether he survived because of an act of mercy, or because his survival was necessary to the over-all plan, or because the fruit had been forbidden him in order that, forsaking the enervations of Eden, he should assert his human recalcitrance — all such speculations are irrelevant for present purposes. The point is that, though the prohibition was violated, the sanction was not put into effect in the form previously announced. Theoretically Adam was either a lawbreaker or not a lawbreaker; the " law of excluded middle " leaves no other possibility. Is it then the part of wisdom for us, his descendants, to drive out the middle possibility from our social concerns as Adam was driven forth from his garden of ease?

Granted that the jural scene may be easier to understand when philosophers paint it in bold primary colors, nevertheless the shadings and gradations of legal fact look more like exceedingly subtle chiaroscuro. We have to allow for group agitations and compromises, for popular resistances and the open and tacit adjustments that go on in courts and administrative agencies, for pigheaded juries and corrupt judges, and, above all, for lawlessness and crime that somehow and to some degree do pass undetected or unpunished. Too many instances of impunity will, of course, weaken a system of legal order. But what could be more dangerous to it than an ever-literal, austere, relentless enforcement? Revolutions would occur more often than they do if legal discipline were not everywhere tempered by incomplete enforcement; *i.e.*, by what, pursuant to the law of excluded middle, would be denominated lawbreaking. So it is that intelligent legal administration, far from imitating the " obstinate and ignorant tyrant " which Plato criticized, can resemble an understanding parent who sometimes does not know and sometimes prefers not to know that his sternest rules are being infringed.

This recalcitrance of the life of law — this refusal to follow the neat patterns of theory — we may call *the intrusive middle*. It blunts those sharp dichotomies that are so convenient to dialecticians and may also be, as in the case of Biblical King Saul, so lethal to the credulous. Saul naïvely believed that he had lost his charisma and that the law had become impotent to help him, because forsooth he had on a single occasion transgressed its command. He believed that to disobey the law is to " break " it (a mere play on words), and that mistaken belief brought him to despair and ruin. He should have been assured that the law is more resilient and flexible.

This characteristic flexibility in applying the law would be less necessary if we were not all nonconformists on one score or another. Since such we are, the intrusive middle proves a boon to the operative sense of injustice. The rationality that it informs is not indifferent to diversities in human society or incapable of recognizing incompleteness and causal pluralism when it witnesses them. Particularly can it serve to chasten those dogmatists, in or out of government, whose adamant consistency would have killed Adam forthwith and ended the species once and for all.

Men's cabins — in whatever acceptation we may choose to regard the term — are centers and headquarters of the intrusive middle. The cabin makes the regime of law possible because there, if anywhere, the austere *either-or's* are transmuted into *both-and's* and occasionally into *neither's*. There, if anywhere, government can help to relieve the gloom without taking possession of the premises; there law (with its particularization of guilts based on objective action and its absolutions) can alleviate men's burdens without dwarfing their individualities. Thus the legal system can contribute to make the cabin viable and its owner secure in his society. But all this requires a certain conceived humility on the part of government and a firm, general insistence that legal action subserve the claims of particular desert.

The Rail as Safeguard. Perhaps we should be less insistent on being judged according to particular desert if each of us thought better of his own general desert. Everyone suspects — at times he knows — that an objective report of his entire inner life would include certain festers and suppurations. This knowledge or half-awareness may cover itself with diffidence or may dress itself in pride and aggressive demandings; in either case the cloak appears uncomfortably thin, at least to the one who wears it. The inadequacies underneath remain discernible and sometimes they seem exaggerated by the very effort to mask them

But they would be even more evident and more painful if the law of citizenship did not afford some measure of participative security. Though nothing else furnishes support, the national political structure stands like a solid protecting rail.

The feel of this protection is probably at its firmest when the citizen goes abroad. However unimportant he may seem at home, he carries a part of his nation's dignity as he travels outside its borders. Under the law of nations, he finds in himself the equal of any other citizen. The question then is: When he returns to his own country, can he find there too that national citizenship is an operative force for human equality?

It is unsafe to generalize about a phenomenon so protean as the politically organized nation. This structural form is very old and, in its present manifestations, very new. In certain functions it has recently attained what seems like an apogee of social utility; in others it appears to have been waning for several generations. The diversity of its manifestations from continent to continent is notorious. But there is at least one attribute that seems to characterize the nation almost everywhere: it builds and maintains its outer rails around some species of community.

Whether the community or its national political safeguards came first in the historic order is immaterial to the interests of the individual citizen. He finds them existing together and reacting upon each other, and he will remain unaware of any distinction between them unless their respective standards should seem to conflict in some radical respect. In his experience, the nation is simply the largest of his social groups, one that operates to expand the bounds of his loyalties and his conformities throughout an immense geographic area. Without it, he would see no necessary connection to men in distant cities or on isolated farms or in unfamiliar pursuits. The nation widens his sympathies and gives him new occasions for pride. A citizen in Maine or RSFSR is enabled to perceive his counterpart in the Californian or the Uzbek.

The national community enfolds a congeries of overlapping lesser communities. Into these we are born; they form the shape of our growth; they give us our mores and most of our standards of value. The national political force encircles the whole with its protection, keeping it safe and firm. If we cherish any substantial part of the positive social structure which has molded our lives (complacency, habit, and inertia make us likely to cherish it beyond its merits), we will prize the strong outer rail that keeps us securely aboard and closes off the foreign and the unaccustomed. And the existence of the rail serves as an admonition to respect and find communion with all those on the inner side.

National communities engage in enterprises that embody, at least in some partial manner, the values they have learned to emphasize. The particular enterprise may be a war of defense or aggression, the building of an electric power dam, the replacement of slums, the defeat of disease, the control of economic cycles, or the dissemination of political ideals believed to be orthodox. The citizen who is summoned along with all the rest to contribute his money, services, or blood to a national enterprise may experience a new, intense, exhilarating sensation of participative security. If the enterprise is such as to appeal to his sense of injustice, *i.e.*, if the ills it seeks to remove for others are such that he can empathize them as a menace to himself, he can exhibit undiscovered forces of courage, zeal, and dedication. If he can be convinced that he is serving not merely an undertaking but a principle, he will forget all divisive fears and hasten to the ranks. For the community's sense of injustice has a stupendous drive. As Thomas Paine described it: " An army of principles will penetrate where an army of soldiers cannot; it will succeed where diplomatic management would fail; it is neither the Rhine, the Channel nor the Ocean that can arrest its progress. It will march on the horizon of the world, and it will conquer." [17]

The Rail as Threat of Rejection. Now it is time to look at the other side of the rail, its outer side. Its strength and sustenance are believed to be derived from the fact that, having an outer side, it can close off what is unknown and unsafe. At the rail social support has its margins, and beyond these there is nothing but a sort of juridical abyss. The richer and securer the group life on this side of the rail, so much the more ominous will that abyss seem to those who falter at its edge. They have correspondingly much to lose in the rejection and the fall.

To deport an undesirable inhabitant is, of course, to thrust him physically over the rail; but, as deportation is more commonly applied in these times not to citizens but to aliens, the example it affords would be somewhat exceptional. Unfortunately, we do not lack more representative instances, instances of that kind of radical reduction in the rights of citizenship which the Roman law called *capi-*

[17] Final paragraph of Agrarian Justice.

tis deminutio. These instances illustrate either physical ostracism on the one hand or civic demotion on the other, and they may be inflicted on citizens who ostensibly remain within the bounds of the national society. The infamies of this sort perpetrated in despotic polities need no listing; it will be more instructive to concentrate on recent occurrences within democratic legal systems.

Banishment is a cruel form of punishment, but in centuries past it was alleviated by the receptive attitude of other countries, some of which could offer at least as much comfort and culture and more freedom of expression than the homeland. This alleviation was not available during the halcyon days of Rome, for, as Gibbon points out, there was only starvation or murder by savage tribes awaiting one who passed beyond the imperial frontiers.[18] So it was that the penalty of exile at that time had to be endured within the jurisdiction of the same sovereign who had decreed it and who could be counted on to maintain or increase its severity.

This is the species of internal exile that has become frequent in the present era. Soon after the attack on Pearl Harbor, the United States not only forcibly transported aliens of Japanese ancestry (whom it had by statute denied the privilege of naturalization) from their California homes to distant internment camps in the interior; it further imposed a discriminatory curfew regulation on all American citizens of such ancestry residing along the Pacific Coast.

[18] Fichte, influenced perhaps by the *interdictio aquae et ignis* of the Roman Republic, permitted imposition of the death penalty but insisted that the criminal could be executed only by being expelled from the state. Cairns, Legal Philosophy from Plato to Hegel 480 (1949). The same device has been used by peoples whom we recognize as primitive. Coon, A Reader in General Anthropology 460 (1948).

These fiats were defended in the ineffable name of military necessity, and the Supreme Court, although evincing certain twinges of uneasiness, unanimously upheld the action.[19] This segment of the rail began then to feel weak to those who leaned on it and a year later it collapsed. In the *Korematsu* case the Court majority sustained the conviction in a civil court of a native American citizen of Japanese ancestry who had boldly remained in his home instead of reporting for detention and removal.[20] In this manner, citizens of a specific class were stigmatized, constricted, and interned within the land of their birth, not because of anything they had said or done, but because of a racial imputation on the part of the military.

There is a subtler version of *capitis deminutio*, which now affects the citizenry of every industrialized nation. The threat is an old one but its ubiquity and power are something new. It has to do with what the Greeks meant by *hybris* or the Romans by *actio injuriarum aestimatoria* [21] when understood in terms of " the insolence of office." The social-welfare state, whether regulating or owning the productive resources of its people, must administer them through a numerous and increasingly powerful civil service. Unless the legal order takes suitable precautions, most of the wielders of these novel authorities are destined to conduct themselves like all other potentates, that is, haughtily, rudely, injuriously. Even a civil servant clothed

---

[19] Hirabayashi v. United States, 320 U. S. 81 (1943).

[20] Korematsu v. United States, 323 U. S. 214 (1944).

[21] Remedies for affronts and acts of contumely have not been confined to ancient law. For example, they are known to Scots law and to Roman-Dutch law. We need to recognize that money damages will not salve the kind of wounds that a civilian or military bureaucrat may inflict. We need new and cogent versions of the *amende honorable*.

like a monarch in the splendid robes of socialist sovereignty should be required to consider whether he does not owe respect to every citizen who approaches him in his official capacity. The point is that our traditional laws and procedures governing redress against officials appear increasingly ineffectual and outmoded. We need and shall need more sorely: expeditious departmental regulations and reviews; judicial and administrative remedies for oppressiveness, negligence, and delay; and, above all, new concepts of torts arising out of contumely or humiliation. Socialism cannot hold itself above other tenure systems if in daily operation it compels citizens to wait hat in hand or deprives them of honor and self-regard. In so far as state ownership of enterprise may appear appropriate, the legal and administrative orders are under duty to maintain a socialism-with-pride.

The Rail as Barrier. Those on either side of the rail have a way of regarding their side as the inner, the safe, and the exclusively desirable. The crimes and follies consequent on chauvinism and xenophobia are too obvious to need mention here. As the nation-state gradually recedes in efficacy before the progress of the international society, it exacts an increasing toll of anxiety and oppression. Nevertheless, it does seem slowly to move toward its fitting secondary function in world affairs. Within the scope of our present study, there is room only for the curt conjecture that an international state will come into being through the progressive delegation to it of more and more specialized functions of government, that the outward show of national independence will be indefinitely preserved, and that when the time comes to surrender the most tenacious symbols of external sovereignty they will ring so hollow as to be scarcely worth retaining.

In the meanwhile the sense of injustice continues to cross national boundaries and to inspire imaginative interchange with the peoples of every continent. It does not await the tedious installation of adequate juridical machinery, but works as best it can with that at hand. In its manifestations human dignity is a value that may be recognized and felt despite the positive diversity in languages, cultures, or passing national interests. When the global state does ultimately appear, that consummation may be due as much to development of the sense of injustice in each of the coalescing nations as to any other cause or combination of causes.

The reason is a very reassuring one. The insecurity suffered by the individual citizen is due largely to his lack of control over forces so remote as his government and its arsenal. He fears the blunders and offenses that his own government and its allies may commit; the aggressions of a potential enemy he has steeled himself to resist at any necessary cost. But his only hope of influencing so gigantic an enterprise as foreign relations is to ally himself with innumerable others. This the public sense of injustice enables him to do. Others, perceiving the same threat he perceives, voice the same resentment and claim the same inherent dignity. All such are his true allies. Many of them, he may be certain, live under the flag that his own government happens to fear.

Culmination. When we examined the cabin as part of man's social support afforded by law, we arrived at certain reasonably persuasive judgments. At least it became apparent that, *unless* law abides by particular desert and respects the privacy of personality and residence, it can convey no assurance of security. Now our view from either side of the rail supplies one or two additional conclusions. We learn that *unless* human dignity is recognized and upheld in domestic and in international law, unless it transcends the rail that any temporal occasion may erect, our anxieties will not be laid to rest.

And now suppose that all we have sought in the hull and the keel, the cabin and the rail were earnestly striven for. Suppose that a determined and general demand were voiced for honest judges and limited human liabilities, for provision of continuity in experience, for active equality in the sharing of social accessions, for passive equality in sustaining social burdens, for admeasurements by law according to particular desert, for respect of privacy of personality and residence, and for protection of human dignity on every continent. Suppose that we resolve to undertake all these beneficences — then at last would we be secure?

IV. *The Chart and the Motive Power*

This is the ultimate question and, in order to confront it intelligently, we need to recapitulate the steps we have traversed and to ascertain where we find ourselves. We began our study of " Justice and Power " with a decision of abnegation. At the outset it appeared that any abstract formula we might derive by using the traditional techniques of rational deduction or induction would prove vain and indefensible. All such avenues which so many have attempted before us seemed to lead by one way or another to a dead end. So we decided rather to base our progress on that which each of us could observe in his own daily experience, could feel in his body and know in his mind: the sense of injustice. Its manifestations are reassuringly familiar to anyone who candidly examines the content of his own consciousness.

We recognized, of course, that a variety of positive influences would affect the reactions and the synaptic paths of any given individual, because each of us is in large measure the product of his specific biography and of the society in which he lives. And, necessarily, the blend of reason and emotion within the sense of injustice precluded any pretense of sweeping juristic generalizations applicable always and everywhere. These are admonitory considerations, which we have endeavored to keep before us. The permutations and oscillations of the positive must be taken into account, and by and large it is the refusal to take them into account that has defeated many undertakings similar to ours. But why may they not be taken adequately into account, if instead of seeking to draft a list of sloganlike maxims we pursue the understanding of each partly familiar, partly novel case as it develops and unreels? The sense of injustice is only one of the several causes that are *constitutive* of particular answers; to find it permanently *constituted* in any single answer or series of answers (not excluding such as may have been proffered in these pages) is to betray it.

Ideals and Incarnations. For those who innocently commit this error the betrayal is almost certain to prove costly. Juristic precepts, if taken as literal descriptions of positive law in action, may be so remote from the observable phenomena that the expectations they raise are likely to terminate in disillusionment. The onlooker sees lofty ends committed to the ministry of dubious means; he notices that what is done often makes a caricature of what is said. At numerous points and positions the chart published by his society seems to belie the coast he can quite clearly see; and so, losing confidence in the announced bearings, he may suffer a kind of panicky bewilderment.

The sense of injustice has a latent capacity to reduce such psychic sufferings. We notice that it arises only to meet the challenge of the here-and-now, the real or imagined haecceity of the occasion. It responds to each human predicament as ultimately important. This here-and-nowness shows the incarnation of ideal standards in the variable flesh of circumstance. On each unique juncture of values and events, the sense of injustice focuses its concern; this and no other is its time and place to succeed as far as possible or to fail. The disillusionments men experience come from looking for justice in mansions, where it is not to be found, instead of at street corners where it makes its appearance. *That* justice is we know before the occasion, but only the occasion discloses precisely *what* it calls on us to do.

Facets, Freedom, and Fear. The occasions have not, however, proved hopelessly disparate. They seem to fall into certain crude groupings (not categories) which we denominated " facets " of the sense of injustice. These facets included the demands for equality, for desert, for human dignity, for conscientious adjudication, for confining of government to its proper functions, and for fulfillment of common expectations. We found that each of these effected a working difference in the formal rules and individual applications of positive law; in short, that the sense of injustice participates *ad hoc* in shaping general rules of law and specific judgments.

When we came to consider the species of human mobility which is called " freedom," we discovered that it involved a series of tacit assumptions concerning man, truth, and law. Those assumptions seemed to float out of reach of earth, until we observed how the sense of injustice, like a sturdy cable, held them down and maintained their connection with the native capacities of men. Once identified, this nexus between human biological equipment and the conditions of legal mobility gave us courage to analyze the operations of law for their pedagogic values. At the end, we concluded that law could assist men to make themselves ready for autonomous life. Though only a possibility, it was one to quicken the beat of the blood.

And now we who have been looking for the sources of security are prepared to face our ultimate question. We have learned that there is no lasting social support in the absence of such requisites as honest judges or respect for privacy. But to speak of honest judges is to evoke our familiar facet of " conscientious adjudication," and the need for privacy necessarily involves " confinement of government to its proper functions." So too with the indispensable passive and active " equality," particular " desert," and protection of " human dignity "; they likewise are facets of the sense of injustice. Finally, there is the requisite of limited liabilities and of continuity in human experience, which corresponds rather closely to the facet called " fulfillment of common expectations." Thus every single facet of the sense of injustice is involved in our culminative question. A few pages back, we asked whether striving for a certain combination of beneficences would make us at last secure. Now, in the light of this recapitulation, we may put the inquiry more closely: If we heed the sense of injustice, then could we expect to be secure? Would obedience to the sense of injustice supply us with firm footing, with social support?

On Behalf of the Adversary. At the start it must be conceded that there is much to say on behalf of that shrewd personage whose aim it is to convince men that their undertakings are as futile as those of beasts of the field. He calls himself " der Geist der stets verneint," and by long experience in insinuating the worthlessness of attempts to execute justice he has become an expert dialectician. Moreover, he knows how to talk the language of our times.

Here he would begin by calling attention to the numberless species of insecurity to which the legal order is entirely unrelated. A person may pass through the years of his life in a state of feverish anxiety because his father has tyrannized over him, or his mother has given him excessive protection, or because his schooling was deficient, or because the one he loves most holds him in contempt. Can the law reverse the work of Circe and convert the squeal of such frightened pigs into the rational speech of men?

After elaborating the themes of current psychology, he would turn to the pages of the economists. There he would select a variety of possible grounds for doubt and disbelief. What good can the sense of injustice accomplish if the country fails to yield what its population requires? The first sharp pinch of necessity would make men forget the twinges of injustice; and, it must be admitted, the majority of human beings on the face of the earth have always been and today remain necessitous.

Then there are certain views of anthropology and sociology which likewise may be made to support the argument that security flows like grains of dry sand through men's fingers. Cultures, we are told, are alike only in their infinite diversity, their utter incommensurability. What our society happens to recommend is our meat; what it dislikes is our poison. It presents us with its particular set of standards, shapes us to accept them, and punishes every effort at departure and innovation. These being the facts of social existence, the sense of injustice could operate only by incorporating patterns of behavior that the particular group had already taught. An act consistent with the approved pattern could not possibly be reacted to as a wrong.

And now the argument moves to attack on the home soil of our own exposition. At the outset, were we not compelled to grant the impossibility of knowing that any specific challenge to the sense of injustice had been fully understood by men's reason or comprehended in imaginative interchange? The currents of causation flow and divide and meet endlessly again; it is beyond the power of the wisest to mark where reflection, sympathy, and analysis may properly stop. A security founded on appreciation of some necessarily truncated part of the case may prove deceptive indeed.

Moreover, the very modesty of our conclusions shows how little of marrow they can lay claim to. The most we have dared to deduce is that there can be no security for all members of the community *unless* certain conditions of juristic order are constructed. Granted that these conditions closely parallel the objectives of the sense of injustice; granted that whatever impairs these conditions calls the sense of injustice into exercise: there was nothing in the exposition to show that various other circumstances are not equally potent to establish or to shatter the platform of social support. Our survey has simply denied that security can be achieved without the practice of justice. True, this argument affords some kind of effective threat to those who are unjust; as for the just, they seem to be left where they were before, except that they lack the fragile gains and gaudy baubles which injustice may proffer.

This brings the Adversary to an ancient and familiar thesis, one that has had centuries of constant use in the theological arena. He insists that there is no demonstrable connection between justice on the one hand and success on the other (that is, unless " justice " is nothing more than an honorific title for whatever conduct happens to be followed by profit in the particular case). Of course, credulous humans may choose to believe that the web of existence comprises a thread to bind just action and effectuality together; in fact, some of them embrace this illusion with such superstitious gullibility that they become embarrassed by every natural and unavoidable misadventure, arguing in their subconscious illogic that it must somehow imply a defect of virtue. But all this is sheer obscurantism and folly. The rational observer learns from incontrovertible evidence, too overwhelming to be ignored, that chance may favor or mischance afflict the culprit as well as the just, and that success and failure are never recognized in the appearance of their seeds.

Thus it is that the Adversary presents his case. And assuredly the total effect of the analysis might well insinuate despair into sanguine minds. Much that he has said is worth remembering, if only to limit the claims of the sense of injustice to their proper province and to forestall the frauds that follow from shallow optimism. But to limit claims is not to surrender them, and we are hardly ready yet to concede the utter vanity of our grand enterprise. For in the teeth of precisely such objections as those epitomized here, Isocrates insisted that " they are of all men most afflicted with unreason who concede that justice is a way of life more noble and more pleasing to the gods than injustice but at the same time believe that those who follow it will live in worse case than those who have chosen the way of evil." [22]

On Behalf of Justice. We who consider ourselves not " afflicted with unreason " will press on to inspect these several objections and to ascertain whether the answers to them may be discovered. In that undertaking we must center our analysis on considerations arising out of the place and time in which any specific human predicament arises and becomes vivid in experience. The sense of injustice finds its sanctions, if any it has, in the focus of times, places, and circumstances. Only in such terms is its utility asserted in our exposition; hence only thus will it be refuted or sustained.

If we are to argue on behalf of justice rationally as well as passionately (both are fitting), we should recall attention to the meaning that was attributed to security throughout this study. Security, we agreed, is for our purposes

[22] On the Peace 35 (Loeb's trans. 1929), II, 31.

the feel of firm social support, and insecurity the sensation of weakness or possible withdrawal of social support. Of course, there are other important acceptations of security and insecurity, other means by which one may draw strength or lose it. Without disparaging them, we are warranted in insisting that they are outside the scope of this inquiry and pragmatically irrelevant to the influences of law. The sense of injustice, though subtle, does not pretend to remedy insecurities that may arise out of exceedingly intimate experiences such as those in the womb, at the breast, or in the connubial bed. On the other hand, we have seen that it can reduce the burden of guilts which have a societal origin; it can furnish an assurance of mutual solidarity and protection; and it can push out the horizons of individual personality. That it cannot do all things is simply an additional voucher of its fitness for a finite cosmos.

The objections purported to be based on economic and sociological data are of more serious weight. Though hungry men and women do frequently conduct themselves with astonishing discipline and consideration, there is no use claiming that the sense of injustice is a fair substitute for comestibles or for clothing and shelter. Hunger corrodes all social bonds; it would be idle to argue that people who have little or nothing to eat can feel themselves secure. Nevertheless, the Adversary's argument, when rightly understood, sustains rather than refutes the efficacy of the sense of injustice. For what are the demands for equality, for fulfillment of common expectations, and for human dignity when applied *ad hoc* but the first great impulsions to apportion and share supplies of food, clothing, and other necessaries? The sense of injustice does not itself satisfy the gastric juices, but it can and visibly does, in times and places, initiate plans and methods to have them satisfied. If the abundant products of the soil are ultimately made to supply every living individual's consumptive needs, that achievement will be due to an awakened sense of injustice throughout the unlimited human community. Until then we shall be compelled to admit the existence of embarrassing flaws and apertures in the platform of social support. It would be wise, in the interest of our own security, to anticipate, by imaginative interchange, the resentment and outrage of those who are hungry.

The suffering that comes from hunger does serve to show how far the Adversary has overstated the implications of sociological method. Protracted hunger is an experience which no culture, however eccentric, has yet taught the general mass of its population to enjoy. And there are other experiences of the same ubiquitous nature — having to do with the existence, sustenance, and protection of the body, the opportunity to move about, to copulate, to assert and develop personality. Disparities of mores and cultural idiosyncrasies, though fascinating to observe and catalogue, need not obscure the similarities and parallelisms in social experience. For societies have to face much the same organizational problems, though some of them discover what we may consider peculiar solutions. Marriage customs, for example, may vary on many scores, but are they not all improvised answers to the same questions (those arising out of the primitive data of sex, cohabitation, gestation, child bearing and nurture, pubescence, family labor, etc.)?

Then, of course, there is the striking answer afforded by the very existence of the science of sociology. If each man's values were wholly and exclusively predetermined to be those of his own society, who could stand off from his group and appraise it against a measuring rod of objectivity? Who could criticize this standard or that? Who could denounce the social order in which he grew, or the institutions which are alleged to have shaped his judgment so irrevocably? The capacity to denounce the familiar indicates the existence and activity of something even more familiar; *i.e.*, the sense of injustice correctly or mistakenly applied.

Yes, that much is true: the sense of injustice may be and frequently is applied mistakenly. And even when its exercise is correct according to the measure of the known facts, certain critical data may not be known or may not yet exist to become susceptible of knowledge. Chance may and does intervene to frustrate judgment and confound the plans of the wise; such is the way of our universe. We cope with an endless concatenation of causes and accidents, for the sufficient reason that we must work with what we have. But, working with it, we can slowly learn to record some of the habits of its vicissitudes and to manipulate them with cumulative craftsmanship. The enterprise is always difficult; at times it is disconcerting; less obdurate creatures would have long since abandoned it. But somehow in the unremitting test we occasionally receive intimations of advancement, and then we can say with Albert Einstein: " God is sophisticated, but he is not malicious."

Reason does not require that we distrust the sense of injustice whenever supervening events cause it in a particular instance to fall short of its goal. If it were exempt from the possible interferences of future factors, it would probably prove less useful in disposing effectually of those at hand in the present. Its biological occasion is the here-and-now, to which reason and empathy conjointly make their response. The future, it admonishes, is neither wholly ours nor wholly beyond our resolution to manipulate. When some new occurrence invalidates an appreciation formed by the sense of injustice, then we are entitled to call Hume's observation to mind: "Why is this peach-tree said to be better than that other, but because it produces more or better fruit? And would not the same praise be given it, though snails or vermin had destroyed the peaches before they came to full maturity?"[23]

We have said there is no lasting security without exercise of the sense of injustice. This conclusion was itself a most impressive reassurance, because it made the active pursuit of justice a condition *sine qua non* of social support. To the Adversary that seemed hopelessly little, but to men, that is to say, to creatures endowed with the sense of injustice, it is enough to lift the heart. For if the argument stopped at this point, and went no farther, it would still be sufficient to stigmatize every tyranny, every social abuse, and every usurpation of power as congenitally insecure and corrosive of the security of others. Is this by itself a mean conclusion?

We are, however, not yet in port. In order to complete our journey, it is necessary to consider once more the

[23] From a footnote to Section V, part ii, of An Enquiry Concerning the Principles of Morals (1740).

biological purpose served by the sense of injustice. That purpose is the repelling of assaults, sometimes immediately experienced, sometimes brought to immediacy by the miracle of imaginative interchange. The experience of the sense of injustice is itself the greatest of all species of social transformation, because it incites men to join with one another and to participate — first in the perception of jeopardy, then in the resistance, and finally in the exultations of an achieved success. These are all public acts of solidarity.

In the cohesiveness of these acts lies our ultimate answer to the Adversary. Perhaps, as he has always said, the rain does fall on the just and the unjust alike, and there is absolutely nothing in the providential order of the cosmos to furnish rewards for the doing of justice. Yet even so his thesis stands confounded before the facts of societal experience. For we have seen that *justice as a working process creates its own cumulative rewards* in every emergent occasion. Among these are freedom, cohesion, and mutual confidence, which each of us may join in attaining both for himself and for his congeners.

We are offered no categorical warranty; how amid the ways of this world should we come to the state of expecting one? There is only the certain opportunity that men may, through exercise of the sense of injustice, draw closer and become everywhere increasingly secure. " The work of justice," [24] we have been told, " shall be peace; and the effect of justice, quietness and assurance forever." Forever? No, surely not forever, but until the sense of injustice stirs once more and calls men again to gird themselves.

[24] Isaiah 32.17.

A PERSONAL EPILOGUE

For me philosophy did not begin, as the Greeks used to say, with wonder but with a condition of acute unease. Two harsh problems had sunk their barbs in me and I had to find a way to cope with them. This is how I came to write *The Sense of Injustice*.

It was in the spring of 1945 that the pressure reached a climax. Hitler and his forces had been defeated at last, World War II was visibly drawing to a close, and men could permit themselves to pause and reflect again, ask the big, long-term questions again, raise their eyes from the duties and terrors of the war and try again to decipher some larger designs and deeper meanings. Anyone who did stop and gaze at the general human scene was sure to feel badly shaken. If the old landmarks had not entirely disappeared, they had been battered and altered and disfigured beyond recognition.

Everything we thought we knew in 1933 when Hitler came to power had to be located and learned anew. He had proved, his Germany had proved that what we had been walking on with confidence, assuming it was bedrock beneath our feet, was in reality the thin treacherous cover of a live volcano. He taught us to acknowledge that the old familiar assumptions we had always trusted were conclusively, permanently, desperately unsafe. And amid our fears and confusions we heard voices everywhere insisting that military power was the only ground for nations to stand on and that the only way to preserve law and order, government and society was to possess preponderant might and rely on organized force.

In those days if a man felt—as I did—that the cult of force was too repugnant to be accepted uncritically and that, even in the new age of distrust, government and law might have other meanings for human beings, what other meaning could he find without indulging in self-deception? I had to search.

My second problem, the one that was personal and my own, served to intensify the search. I had entered my fortieth year, a difficult stocktaking period for a man in almost any circumstances and, in my instance, painfully difficult. When I reflected that I had been practicing law for some eighteen years by that time, that I continually talked and argued in and out of court about "justice," that I often contended that justice was the goal and purpose of legal institutions in general and of my own vocation in particular, and when I realized that I still could not explain intelligibly what I meant by the word, I felt ashamed. Eighteen years a practicing lawyer (there would be another five years before I became a full-time teacher) and I could not explain the one word that made sense of my professional life.

Of course, I had seen the need and exerted some efforts before 1945. For years I had read, listened, studied, studied, listened, and read; in course of time I got full without being satisfied. It seemed as though I knew what everyone since the sixth century B.C. had to say about justice—everyone, that is, save only myself. What would it avail to continue quoting Aristotle or Whitehead, Thomas Aquinas or William James? Did I agree with them, disagree with them, or have a view of my own? It was *my* career, *my* life that must somehow be accounted for.

Although *The Sense of Injustice* is a short book, it required about four years to write. It took so long not because I was very busy—though indeed I was—with law practice, legal scholarship, civil liberties endeavors and other public duties, but because I was simply unable to think the problems through in a briefer span of time.

No sooner had the book been published than my students in jurisprudence and philosophy of law, most of whom were practicing lawyers, began to scrutinize and probe and question it not only to understand what I was propounding but also to uncover their own ethical convictions and assess their own professional careers. The questions, I noticed, tended to repeat themselves year after year as one group of readers after another would meet the same unexpected passages and arrive at the same moral crossroads.

It occurs to me that it would be an interesting idea to record the main questions along with the substance of my usual answers. Why not? At least they may prevent some possible misunderstanding and help to make my purposes clear. Here are the ones that recur most regularly:

Q. In this book are you trying to provide a formula of natural laws or a fixed hierarchy of values to govern the handling of particular transactions or the deciding of particular cases?

A. Neither, because there is no such formula or fixed hierarchy available to any human being who exercises his intelligence freely. A free and mature mind understands that when it confronts moral choices and decisions, it cannot find ready-made "answers in the back of the book."

Q. Since you do not subscribe to a natural law philosophy, would it be permissible to summarize your position as "deciding according to one's emotions, intuitions, or viscera"?

A. It would not. The book is explicit about the vital and indispensable role of reason in the rousing of the sense of injustice and the practical functioning of justice.

Q. Now that nearly twenty years have passed since you began the work, would you wish to modify anything you wrote to describe the sense of injustice and its various facets?

A. Yes, I think that in the first chapter when I said that the demand for "conscientious *adjudication*" was one of the facets of the sense of injustice, it would have been wiser to use the more comprehensive phrase "conscientious *official behavior*." While crooked adjudication can rouse the sense of injustice, so too can crooked legislation, crooked administration, or crooked police work.

Moreover, on occasion, a total callousness on the part of officials can be as unjust as dishonesty. For example, even though the legislature of my state may possess constitutional authority and rational warrant for destroying a property interest of mine in order to serve the common good, it would exercise its power unjustly if it simply ignored the existence of my interest and refused to take it into account before reaching a decision.

Q. Do not different individuals reach different and even conflicting positions on events that rouse their sense of injustice?

vigilance and sense of injustice

A. Of course they do. No one would doubt this. But the fact that individuals differ in their reactions does not disparage the existence of the sense of injustice or the reality of its influence in the law. One might as well argue that because men use their reasoning powers and reach different conclusions, there is no such faculty as reason. One might as well argue that because some men lead a miserly life while others make reasonable provisions for the future and still others squander their last cent, there is no such value as prudence. One might as well argue that because different men are drawn to different women, there is no such impulsion as sex. Unanimity is not the test of a social phenomenon. Coercion can bring about the appearance of unanimity in a group; the voluntary surrender of intellectual freedom can also provide a semblance of unanimity; but wherever men act as free citizens of a free society, some are bound to differ from others in attitudes, intensities, opinions and judgments.

When men differ over issues that are resolvable by legal or political processes, the constitution of the particular country provides the mechanics for the enactment of a governing rule. For example, it may declare that a majority vote shall be binding. This does not mean that the majority decision is necessarily right. It does mean that within the area prescribed by the political constitution, the majority are entitled to have their way. The United States Constitution defines certain areas in which the majority are not entitled to have their way, no matter how right they may be.

The formation of a majority on any specific issue is

brought about, at least in part, by public discussion and debate. These processes can refine, graduate, and coalesce the various individual reactions to a public sense of injustice. In a democracy, the public sense of injustice is often irresistible.

Q. If you were not attempting to provide immutable formulas, fixed hierarchies of value, or patterns for unanimous agreement, what were you attempting to establish?

A. That there is a sense of injustice; that it is an active maker and shaper of general laws and particular decisions; and that it can aid the evolution of a state toward the assensual level. These things being so, we are not constrained to join the idolatry of force that has disgraced the twentieth century and put the survival of our species in jeopardy. I submit in all earnestness that the way to gain national security is the same as the way to gain personal freedom. Both are wages of justice.

MIDLAND BOOKS

(continued on next page)

INDIANA UNIVERSITY PRESS
Bloomington

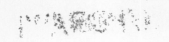